M.Sc. Mario Meister

Ferries on Baltic and North Sea

An overview

Published by:

Northern Aeromarine Ltd.
Westpoint 4 Redheughs Rigg
South Gyle, Edinburgh
EH12 9DQ
United Kingdom

Third actualized edition

ISBN-13: 978-0-9929371-3-3

0.	Contents	Page

Figure 2: M/S Norröna at sea   Photo: © Smyril Line

1. Preface

Ferries are as old as navigation itself. Just the mythology of the ancient world is talking about a ferryman, bringing the souls into the realm of the dead. And in a certain way you can understand also the Noah's Ark as a ferry concept. Until the second half of the 20 century, the ferry ride was limited to the transport of passengers and in lower level, of animals and goods. This changed with the rapid development of transport after World War II and the ever progressive development of the roll-on - roll-off (RO/RO) concept. Now also extensive flows of goods could be moved with trucks and railway over the new ships.

This book includes an overview of the ferry companies, which are travelling in the Baltic and North Sea transport and a short description of their ships. Although attempts were made to make this directory as complete as possible, it can not provide a 100% complete content because the ferry industry is in constant motion, from the change of ownership of vessels until route changes and the restructuring of ferry companies.

This thirth edition include many changes to the first and second edition, published as hardcopy in 2014 and 2015. In these years some shipping lines was going out of business, others sold or modified their ships or simply bought new ones. In the same period also shipping line mergers and the formation of new companies occurred.

Since the title of the book is: "Ferries on the Baltic and North Sea", it has been waived the representation of ferry lines and ships outside of these two territories. Therefore ferry connections and vessels, which are operating in the Irish Sea or on the Atlantic coast, are not included, unless the departure port or the destination is located in the North or Baltic Sea area.

Mario Meister

M.Sc. Mario Meister

2. Ferries – A short technical overview

2.1 Types of ferries

At this point we want to talk only about the sea-going ferries. For that reason we don't take a look to the different shallow water ferry concepts. Today we distinguish between pure passenger ferries (PAX) , which serve exclusively for the transport of passengers (including their four-legged companions) , the so-called RO/RO ferries (Roll On - Roll Off) serving the transportation of goods , a high capacity for trucks and optionally comprise railway waggons and beyond merely have cabins for crew and drivers , as well as because of their importance very common mixed freight/passenger ferries (RO/PAX) that should be considered here more detailed. Most Baltic Sea Ferries and North Sea Ferries are of the mixed type RO/PAX, which means that they carry cargo as well as also passengers. For weight and stability reasons they are charged at first with the much heavier trucks and trailers and then with the cars and passengers. For the same reasons, the placement of the trucks or the railway waggons occurs at larger ferries on the lower deck and above, the cars of the passengers. Some of today's ferries have a touch of cruise ship character, which is of course reinforced by restaurants, shops and spa facilities. The RO/PAX ships offer passengers a comfortable, stress-free and safe way to reach together with their car the desired destination.

Figure 3: Passenger ferry HSC Red Jet 5   Photo: © Editor5807 / Wikimedia Commons CC-BY-SA 3.0

Figure 4: RO/RO-Ferry M/S Finnsky   Photo: © Finnlines

Figure 5: Two typical RO/PAX-Ferries: M/S Peter Pan and M/S Nils Holgersson   Photo: © TT-Line

2.2 Typical construction of a RO / PAX Ferry

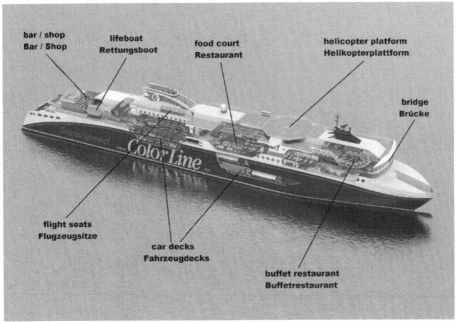

Figure 6: Cutaway HSC SuperSpeed 1   Graphic: © Color Line AS

Figure 7: Cutaway M/S Color Fantasy / Color Magic   Graphic: © Color Line AS

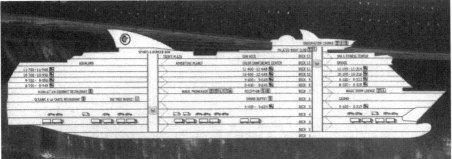

Fifure 8: Layout M/S Color Fantasy / Color Magic   Graphic: © Color Line AS

3. Safety of Ferries

3.1 Fire safety on board of Ferries

Today one of the biggest risks on board of ferries is the risk of fire. This risk arises firstly from the possibility of the occurrence in the engine room by defective fuel and lubricant lines that could ignite and shorts in the electrical system or in the electric motors used. This risk could be minimised by the use of refractory materials and coatings as well as high-efficient fire-fighting equipment. But the main risk of fire on ferries is the cargo itself, the most devastating fire disasters at sea were caused by technical faults on trucks, which were located at the time of the accident on the ship. The problem with fires on ferries, however, is that although the ship is surrounded by water, this water is not available for fire extinguishing. Even if the ship has powerful pumps, the water, pumped into the ship, would lead to a dangerous shift of the centre of gravity upwards and thus increase the risk of capsizing of the ferry considerably. This danger occurs, for example, during the fire of the Hurtigruten ship M/S Nordlys than by the invading fire water a dangerous inclination of the vessel occurred. At this time, however, no more passengers were on board of the "Nordlys". [1]

Figure 9: M/S Nordlys with strong heeling by the inflow of fire-fighting water/Photo: © Elin Støbakk Hald/Wiki Com/CC BY-SA 3.0

A similar situation occurred during the devastating fire on board of the M/S Lisco Gloria, where immense quantities of water were necessary to bring the fire under control and to cool the outer skin of the vessel to prevent a break up of the fuselage. This would have meant a tremendous environmental disaster by oil spills in the sensitive ecological system of the Baltic Sea, particularly near by the island of Fehmarn.[2]

3.2 Why ferries capsizes ?

Accidents involving ferries are rare, but, due to the construction of the ships have serious consequences. In the past, ferries had an undivided vehicle deck to accommodate as many vehicles as possible. This fact, in 1987 led to the disaster of the "Herald of Free Enterprise". The "Herald of Free Enterprise" capsized shortly after to exit the port before Zeebrugge by inflowing sea water, which flowed through the open bow doors into the ship. Thus, a large amount of sea water had the possibility to move from one side to the other in a very short time to shift the centre of gravity of the vessel to the point that it must capsize inevitably. This behaviour is also known under the term "free surface effect." [3]

Centre of gravity in undivided car deck	Centre of gravity (G) in divided car deck

Figure 10: Free Surface Effect   Graphic: © Mario Meister

After the disaster of the "Herald of Free Enterprise" the construction rules for new ferries have been adjusted. It was determined that ferries must have a longitudinally sectioned car deck. Unfortunately, there is to be noted that appropriate safety changes on ferries were always implemented after serious accidents with many victims. So it was in the case of the "Herald of Free Enterprise" as well as the sinking of the "Estonia". Also there water had entered the ship through the torn bow visor and the opening front hatch, which first led to a strong heeling. As additionally the captain conducts a wrong manoeuvre (turning manoeuvre), which subsequently also increased the heel, the fate of the "Estonia" was inevitable,-she capsized and sank little later. [4] Another cause of the capsizing of ferries is the healing of charge, for example, when trucks or rail cars are not secured accordingly and, for example, break loose in a storm and move from one side to the other. Due to the abrupt change of gravity here may arise a critical situation that may lead to the capsizing of the ferry under certain circumstances. For not to let such critical situations end in disaster, modern ferries have a ballast tank system, which allows to restore the balance by counter flooding. This saved a few times the "Jan Heweliusz" before the disaster struck in 1993. Besides complete disregard of weather conditions the "Jan Heweliusz" was not seaworthy at the time and had problems with her ballast compensation system. But the main cause apparently was heeling charge, as apparently one or more poorly secured railway waggons moved and thereby a strong heeling of the ship was the result, which could not be compensated by the defective ballast compensation system and ultimately let capsizing the "Jan Heweliusz". [5]

3.3 Safety instructions for a trouble free crossing [6]

• Find out immediately after arrival at the ferry the nearest collection point (muster station), the position of the life-saving equipment (lifeboats, the drum-shaped containers of liferafts and the usually clearly marked depots with life jackets).

Figure 11: Container with liferafts on board of M/S Tom Sawyer   Photo: © Mario Meister

• Find out how to don a lifejacket! This saves valuable time in an emergency situation and can save your life.

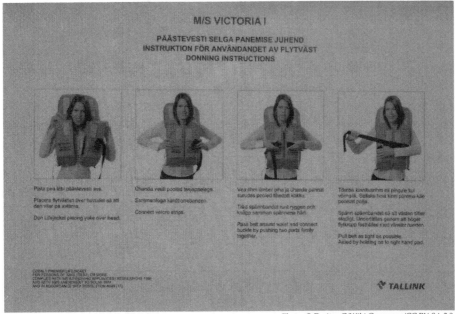

Figure 12: Instructions applying the lifejacket

Photo: © Dmitry G/Wiki Commons/CC BY-SA 3.0

• Please note the absolute ban on smoking on the car deck and in the cabins or the entire ship. Smoking is permitted only in designated passenger areas. Failure to observe this smoking ban can have expensive consequences. Since many areas of the vessel are equipped with smoke detectors that respond to the smoke of a cigarette, the sprinkler system of the corresponding section is active. This means that if you put careless your cabin under water, may be you will be liable for the damage caused by water.

• If you discover a fire or heavy smoke on the ship, immediately notify a member of the crew or press the fire alarm. If you detect near of you a fire extinguisher, you can try to fight the fire. But please be aware not to bring yourself unnecessarily in danger!

• During the crossing, the access to the car deck is strictly prohibited ! This applies from the departure until the arrival at the port of destination, even if the doors to the car deck can be open. Return to your vehicles only after advice from the crew. In an emergency the car deck can become a deadly trap by shifting cargo or vehicles. Since most of the car decks are at the bottom of the vessel, may be in the event of an emergency you don't have enough time to reach the muster stations or the lifeboats.

• In case of emergency applies to ships the same as in buildings: Absolutely do not use elevators ! In the case of fire or power failure these are deadly traps.

• Please do not take any luggage with you exclude valuables and documents. This would impede evacuation in the event of an emergency and bring you and other passengers unnecessarily in danger. The eventual loss of baggage is generally covered by the insurance of the shipping line.

• After the alarm tone sounds, wear warm clothes (if possible) and head soon as possible to the designated collection points (muster station).

Figure 13: Above: Sign for Muster Station / Below: sign for depot lifejackets (20 lifejackets for children + 15 lifejackets for adults)
Photo: © Mario Meister

• First don your lifejacket before you help other passengers. Embark quickly, but without panic the nearest lifeboats or liferafts.

Figure 14: Lifeboats on board of M / S Tom Sawyer   Photo: © Mario Meister

3.4   Short safety review

To make it short, never were ferries safer than today. This is especially valid for the ferries on the Baltic Sea and North Sea. Nevertheless, there are differences in the various ferry lines. This is due to the following factors:

➢ Different professional education and training guidelines

➢ Different levels of professional education

➢ National laws and regulations which differ from IMO and SOLAS regulations

➢ Differences in mentality, which have as consequence a different risk assessment

➢ Different implementation of security standards, which is reflected in more or less incidents during ferry operations

Responsible ferry companies regularly train their personnel on board with emergency drills to ensure a professional handling in the event of an emergency. From time to time also national authorities like port authorities perform an unannounced review of the capabilities of crews in emergency situations in accordance with the provisions of SOLAS. These provisions specify that a ferry in 30 minutes must be evacuated. Therefore, to the former Celtic Link ferry "Norman Voyager" in the North Sea traffic a few years ago was denied the permit to leave the port, because a review showed that the level of training of the crew did not meet the requirements for a safe and fast implementation of the necessary safety measures.[7] Another negative example, with deadly consequences was the disaster of the M/S Estonia in 1994. When the "Estonia" fell into dangerous heeling, the rescue commands of the Estonian crew were given only in Estonian on the central public loudspeaker system and were not understood by the Swedish passengers. [8] This cost valuable time and ultimately thereby many lives.

Figure 15: M/S Estonia   Photo: © CC-0

Even poor technical condition of some ships in the past led to the forced "to put the chain !" A sad example of the consequences of irresponsible neglect of maintenance, with serious implications in turn was the sinking of the "Estonia". In their report the responsible accident investigation commission stated that at the time of the accident the "Estonia" was not seaworthy, maintenance had been criminally neglected and rust had simply been painted over only. This led to the rupture of a locking hinge of the front hatch, which was demolished ultimately by the troubled Baltic Sea.[9] As a result, water entered into the car deck, which led to the capsizing of the ferry at the end. However, this does not mean that every superficial rust is dangerous. So it is normal that, where ferry structures are constantly exposed to the salty sea air and the aggressive salt water of the sea, rusty points are visible. We must not forget that even the best paint reaches its limits in salt water. Therefore, these rust spots are treated professionally during the season break or during maintenance and sealed with a new coat of paint. However, this should not be an excuse for ferry companies and the poor maintenance of their ships as was the case with the Estline with the "Estonia". The IMO was notified of the design problem of the bow visor in various ferries, there was a whole series of incidents and no measures until the disaster struck the "Estonia". [10]

Figure 16: Colorline terminal in Oslo

Photo: © Jørgen Syversen / Firmabilder AS

4.   Shipping companies in the Baltic and North Sea traffic

Shipping companies in the Baltic and North Sea traffic
(November 2017)

Figure 17: Car deck on DFDS ferry

How to read the type directory ?

A short guide

Figure X: NAME OF SHIP (here Figure 18: M/S Barfleur)　　　Photo: © COPYRIGHT OWNER (here © Brittany Ferries)

Name of ship	CURRENT SHIP NAME

Home port / Flag state	PORT OF REGISTRATION / COUNTRY OF REGIST.
Shipyard / Yard number	SHIPYARD, LOCATION, COUNTRY / #NUMBER
Previous ship names	PREVIOUS SHIP NAMES AND PERIODS
Year of construction	YEAR OF COMPLETION

Call sign	IDENTITY CODE	**Classification**	CLASSIF.SOCIETY
IMO Number	PERMANENT ID-NUMBER OF SHIP	**MMSI Number**	COMMUNICATION NUMBER
Length	IN METERS	**Gross tonnage**	GT
Beam	IN METERS	**Net tonnage**	NT
Draught	IN METERS	**Deadweight**	LOADING WEIGHT
Passengers	+BERTHS OR CABINS	**Max. speed**	IN KNOTS
Vehicles	CARS	**Cargo capacity**	IN LANE METERS

Main engines	QUANTITY x MANUFACTURER_TYPE, FUEL / POWER
Auxiliary engines	QUANTITY x MANUFACTURER_TYPE, FUEL / POWER
Propeller	QUANTITY x TYPE, STYLE
Bow thruster	QUANTITY x TYPE, STYLE / POWER

Brittany Ferries

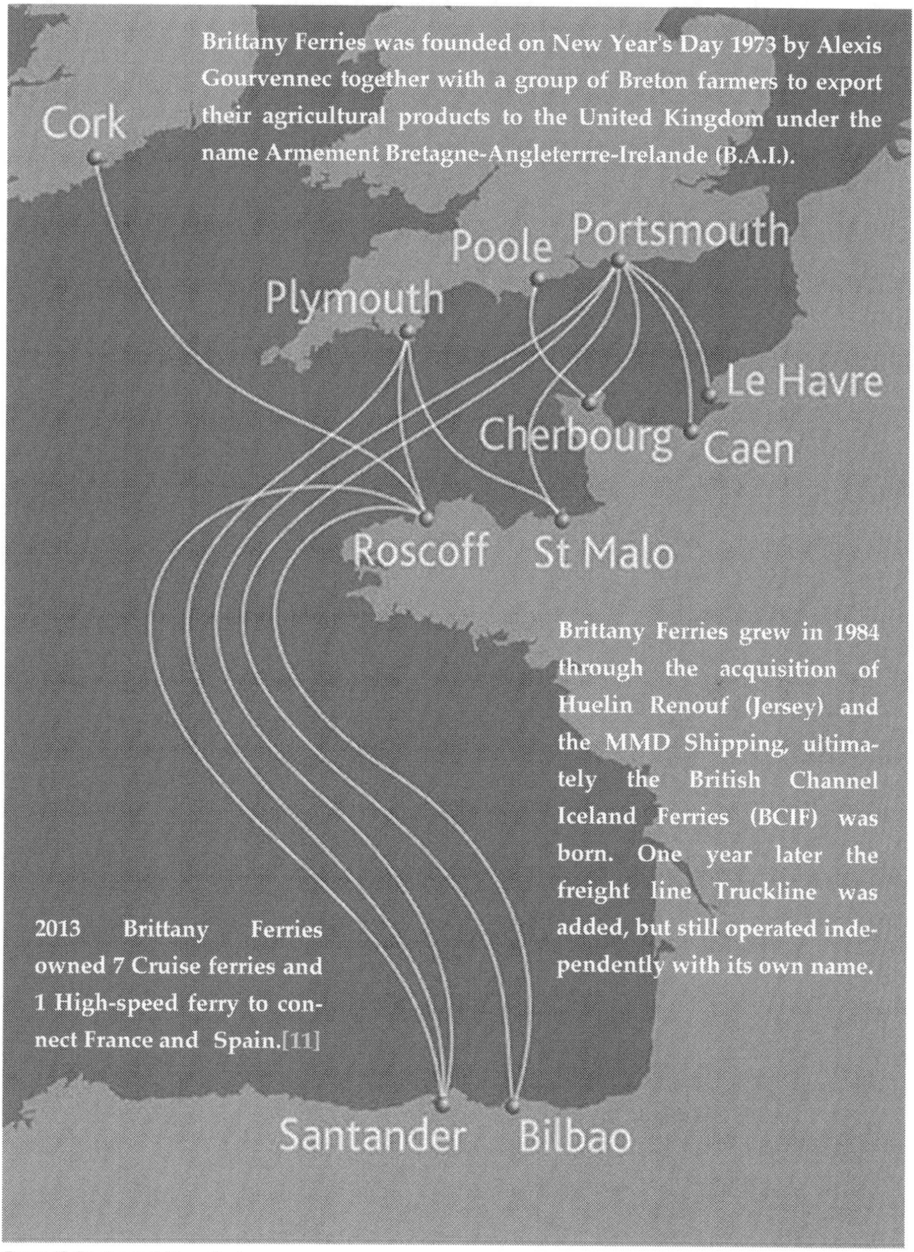

Brittany Ferries was founded on New Year's Day 1973 by Alexis Gourvennec together with a group of Breton farmers to export their agricultural products to the United Kingdom under the name Armement Bretagne-Angleterrre-Irelande (B.A.I.).

Cork

Poole Portsmouth

Plymouth

Le Havre

Cherbourg Caen

Roscoff St Malo

Brittany Ferries grew in 1984 through the acquisition of Huelin Renouf (Jersey) and the MMD Shipping, ultimately the British Channel Iceland Ferries (BCIF) was born. One year later the freight line Truckline was added, but still operated independently with its own name.

2013 Brittany Ferries owned 7 Cruise ferries and 1 High-speed ferry to connect France and Spain.[11]

Santander Bilbao

Figure 19: Routemap Brittany Ferries   Graphic: © Brittany Ferries

Figure 20: M/S Armorique   Photo: © Brittany Ferries

Name of ship   M/S Armorique

Home port / Flag state	Morlais / France
Shipyard / Yard number	STX Europe New Shipyard, Helsinki, Finland / #1362
Previous ship names	-
Year of construction	2009

Call sign	FMLW	Classification	Bureau Veritas
IMO Number	9364980	MMSI Number	228263700
Length	168.30 m	Gross tonnage	29,468 GT
Beam	26.80 m	Net tonnage	11,605 NT
Draught	6.50 m	Deadweight	4,700 tdw
Passengers / Cabins	1,500 / 248	Maximum speed	23 kn
Vehicles	450 Cars	Cargo capacity	980 lm or 55 Trailers

Main engines	2 x MAK 12M43C, Diesel, each 12,000 kW
Auxiliary engines	3 x Wärtsilä 6L20C, Diesel, each 1,140 kW
Propeller	2 x Propeller, controllable pitch
Bow thruster	2 x Tunnel / 1,200 kW and 1 x 900 kW

Figure 21: M/S Baie de Seine   Photo: © Brittany Ferries

Name of ship — M/S Baie de Seine

Home port / Flag state	Le Havre / France
Shipyard / Yard number	Stocznia A.Warskiego, Szczecin, Poland / #B591-1/2
Previous ship names	2002-2002 Golfo Dei Delfini, 2002-2013 Dana Sirena, 2013-2015 Sirena Seaways
Year of construction	2002

Call sign	FISL	**Classification**	Bureau Veritas
IMO Number	9212163	**MMSI Number**	226338000
Length	199.40 m	**Gross tonnage**	22,382 GT
Beam	25.00 m	**Net tonnage**	8,064 NT
Draught	6.32 m	**Deadweight**	5,577 tdw
Passengers / Cabins	600 / 196	**Maximum speed**	23 kn
Vehicles	423 Cars	**Cargo capacity**	2,060 lm

Main engines	2 x Wärtsilä 9L46C, Diesel / each 9,450 kW
Auxiliary engines	3 x ABB AMG 560 S8 / each 1,440 kW
Propeller	2 x Propeller, controllable pitch LIPS
Bow thruster	2 x Tunnel

Figure 22: M/S Barfleur

Name of ship — M/S Barfleur

Home port / Flag state	Cherbourg / France
Shipyard / Yard number	Kvaerner Masa-Yards, Helsinki, Finland / #485
Previous ship names	1992-2012 Barfleur, 2012-2013 Deal Seaways
Year of construction	1992

Call sign	FNIE	**Classification**	Bureau Veritas
IMO Number	9007130	**MMSI Number**	227289000
Length	158.70 m	**Gross tonnage**	20,133 GT
Beam	23.30 m	**Net tonnage**	11,679 NT
Draught	5.80 m	**Deadweight**	5,175 tdw
Passengers / Cabins	1,212 / 72	**Maximum speed**	19.5 kn
Vehicles	590 Cars	**Cargo capacity**	1,530 lm or 75 Lorries

Main engines	4 x Wärtsilä 8R32, Diesel / 12,400 kW
Auxiliary engines	2 x Wärtsilä 8R33/26 - 1,450 kW, 1 x Wärtsilä 6R22/26 - 1,065kW
Propeller	2 x Propeller, controllable pitch
Bow thruster	2 x KaMeWa, each 600 kW

Figure 23: M/S Bretagne   Photo: © Brittany Ferries

Name of ship	M/S Bretagne	

Home port / Flag state	Morlais / France
Shipyard / Yard number	Chantiers de Atlantique, St Nazaire, France / #D29
Previous ship names	-
Year of construction	1989

Call sign	FNBR	**Classification**	Bureau Veritas
IMO Number	8707329	**MMSI Number**	227286000
Length	151.20 m	**Gross tonnage**	24,534 GT
Beam	26.00 m	**Net tonnage**	13,242 NT
Draught	6.20 m	**Deadweight**	3,249 tdw
Passengers / Cabins	2,056 / 376	**Maximum speed**	22.5 kn
Vehicles	580 Cars	**Cargo capacity**	39 Lorries

Main engines	4 x Wärtsilä 12V32E, Diesel / each 4,440 kW
Auxiliary engines	3 x Wärtsilä 6R32 Unelec, Diesel / each 2,250 kW
Propeller	2 x Propeller, controllable pitch
Bow thruster	2 x Tunnel

Figure 24: M/S Cap Finistère

Name of ship — M/S Cap Finistère

Home port / Flag state	Morlais / France
Shipyard / Yard number	Howaldtswerke Deutsche Werft, Kiel, Germany / #355
Previous ship names	2001-2010 Superfast V
Year of construction	2001

Call sign	FLSO	**Classification**	Bureau Veritas
IMO Number	9198927	**MMSI Number**	226318000
Length	203.90 m	**Gross tonnage**	32,728 GT
Beam	25.00 m	**Net tonnage**	13,081 NT
Draught	6.40 m	**Deadweight**	6,515 tdw
Passengers / Cabins	1,608 / 244	**Maximum speed**	27.6 kn
Vehicles	712 Cars	**Cargo capacity**	2,250 lm

Main engines	4 x Sulzer, Diesel / 46,080 kW
Auxiliary engines	3 x Diesel / 1,600 kW
Propeller	2 x Propeller, controllable pitch
Bow thruster	2 x Tunnel

Figure 25: M/S Etretat

Photo: © Brittany Ferries

Name of ship — M/S Etretat

Home port / Flag state	Le Havre / France
Shipyard / Yard number	Cantiere Navale Visentini, Porto Viro, Italy / #220
Previous ship names	2008-2014 Norman Voyager
Year of construction	2008

Call sign	FIDP	**Classification**	Bureau Veritas
IMO Number	9420423	**MMSI Number**	228022900
Length	186.46 m	**Gross tonnage**	26,904 GT
Beam	25.60 m	**Net tonnage**	9,000 NT
Draught	6.80 m	**Deadweight**	7,000 tdw
Passengers / Cabins	800 / 428	**Maximum speed**	23.5 kn
Vehicles	195 Cars	**Cargo capacity**	2,255 lm

Main engines	2 x MAN B&W 9L48/60B, Diesel / 21,600 kW
Auxiliary engines	3 x Diesel / 1,901 kW
Propeller	2 x Propeller, controllable pitch 10.00
Bow thruster	2 x Tunnel

Figure 26: M/S Mont St Michel

Name of ship   M/S Mont St Michel

Home port / Flag state   Caen / France

Shipyard / Yard number   Van der Giessen de Noord, Krimpen, Netherlands / #985

Previous ship names   -

Year of construction   2002

Call sign	FNMT	**Classification**	Bureau Veritas
IMO Number	9238337	**MMSI Number**	227023100
Length	173.95 m	**Gross tonnage**	35,592 GT
Beam	28.50 m	**Net tonnage**	10,677 NT
Draught	6.20 m	**Deadweight**	5,579 tdw
Passengers / Cabins	2,170 / 224	**Maximum speed**	22 kn
Vehicles	830 Cars	**Cargo capacity**	118 Lorries

Main engines   4 x MAK 6M43, Diesel / 21,600 kW

Auxiliary engines   3 x Wärtsilä 9L20C, Diesel / each 1,560 kW

Propeller   2 x Propeller, controllable pitch

Bow thruster   2 x KaMeWa, Tunnel / each 1,500 kW

Figure 27: M/S Normandie   Photo: © Brittany Ferries

Name of ship   M/S Normandie

Home port / Flag state	Caen / France	
Shipyard / Yard number	Kvaerner Masa Yards, Turku, Finland / #1315	
Previous ship names	—	
Year of construction	1992	

Call sign	FNNO	Classification	Bureau Veritas
IMO Number	9006253	MMSI Number	227273000
Length	161.40 m	Gross tonnage	27,541 GT
Beam	26.00 m	Net tonnage	15,760 NT
Draught	6.01 m	Deadweight	5,229 tdw
Passengers / Cabins	2,100 / 220	Maximum speed	20.5 kn
Vehicles	575 Cars	Cargo capacity	1,720 lm or 84 Lorries

Main engines	4 x Wärtsilä 12V23E, Diesel / each 4,440 kW
Auxiliary engines	4 x Diesel / 2,460 kW
Propeller	2 x Propeller, controllable pitch
Bow thruster	2 x Tunnel

Figure 28: HSC Normandie Express   Photo: © Brittany Ferries

Name of ship	HSC Normandie Express	

Home port / Flag state	Caen / France
Shipyard / Yard number	Incat, Hobart, Tasmania, Australia / #057
Previous ship names	2000 Incat Tasmania, 2000-2005 The Lynx
Year of construction	2000

Call sign	FMIH	**Classification**	Bureau Veritas
IMO Number	9221358	**MMSI Number**	228237700
Length	97.22 m	**Gross tonnage**	6,581 GT
Beam	26.60 m	**Net tonnage**	N/A
Draught	3.43 m	**Deadweight**	750 tdw
Passengers / Cabins	850 / No Cabins	**Maximum speed**	42 kn
Vehicles	235 Cars	**Cargo capacity**	No Freight

Main engines	4 x Ruston Paxman 20RK270, Diesel / each 7,080 kW
Auxiliary engines	N/A
Propeller	2 x Waterjet 5.00
Bow thruster	N/A

Figure 29: M/S Pont-Aven
Photo: © Brittany Ferries

Name of ship M/S Pont-Aven

Home port / Flag state	Morlaix / France
Shipyard / Yard number	Meyer-Werft, Papenburg, Germany / #650
Previous ship names	—
Year of construction	2004

Call sign	FNPN	Classification	Bureau Veritas
IMO Number	9268708	MMSI Number	228183600
Length	184.30 m	Gross tonnage	41,700 GT
Beam	30.90 m	Net tonnage	N/A
Draught	6.80 m	Deadweight	4,750 tdw
Passengers / Cabins	2,414 / 652	Maximum speed	27 kn
Vehicles	650 Cars	Cargo capacity	85 Lorries

Main engines	4 x MAK 12V M43, Diesel / 43,200 kW
Auxiliary engines	3 x Wärtsilä 6SW280, Diesel
Propeller	2 x Propeller, controllable pitch Wärtsilä-Lips
Bow thruster	2 x Bow thruster and 1 x Stern thruster

Color Line is a Norwegian shipping company that operates four ferry lines with six ships. It was created in October 1990 by the merger of Jahre Line and Norway Line. In December 1990, Color Line bought the ferry business of Fred. Olsen Lines and in October 1996 the route rights on Larvik Line (Larvik - Frederikshavn). In 1998, Color Line took over the Scandi Line with the M /S Sandefjord, the M /S Bohus and the M /S Color Viking as well as the route rights on the route Strömstad - Sandefjord. Color Line AS is a 100% - subsidiary of the holding company Color Group ASA, Olav Nils Sunde is the sole owner of the Color Line after the acquisition of all shares in November 1998.

Groundbreaking was the commissioning of the M/S Color Fantasy in December 2004 as the "largest cruise ship with a car deck" [quote: Color Line A/S] at this time. The M/S Color Fantasy followed in the fall of 2007 her sister ship, the M/S Color Magic. Another milestone was the opening of the ferry service between Hirtshals and Kristiansand and between the Norwegian Hirtshals and the Danish Larvik with 2 new high-speed ferries , the 211 m long HSC "SuperSpeed 1" and the nearly identical HSC "SuperSpeed 2" in 2008. This reduced the journey times to 3 hours 15 minutes on the route Hirtshals - Kristiansand and to only 3 hours and 45 minutes on the route Hirtshals –Larvik . [12]

Figure 30: Outside environment   Photo: © Dag G. Nordsveen / Nordsveenfoto.no

Figure 31: M/S Bohus

Photo: © Nordsveenfoto.no

Name of ship — M/S Bohus

Home port / Flag state	Sandefjord / Norway
Shipyard / Yard number	Aalborg Vaerft A/S, Aalborg, Denmark / #190
Previous ship names	1971-1982 Prinsessan Desiree, 1983-1985 Europafärjan, 1985-1987 Europafärjan II, 1987-1994 Lion Princess
Year of construction	1971

Call sign	LHDT	Classification	Det Norske Veritas
IMO Number	7037806	MMSI Number	259153000
Length	123.37 m	Gross tonnage	9,149 GT
Beam	19.6 m	Net tonnage	2,744 NT
Draught	5.2 m	Deadweight	1,968 tdw
Passengers / Cabins	1,165 / 126	Maximum speed	21 kn
Vehicles	240 Cars	Cargo capacity	462 lm

Main engines	8 x Nohab Polar SF112 VS-E, Diesel / 11,475 kW
Auxiliary engines	3 x 3512DITA, Caterpillar Inc., Diesel
Propeller	2 x Propeller, controllable pitch KaMeWa CPP 94 S/4
Bow thruster	1 x Tunnel, Rolls-Royce AB

Figure 32: M/S Color Fantasy   Photo: © Fjellanger Wideröe Photo AS

Name of ship   M/S Color Fantasy

Home port / Flag state	Oslo / Norway
Shipyard / Yard number	Kværner Masa Yards AB, Turku, Finland / #1351
Previous ship names	—
Year of construction	2004

Call sign	LMSD	Classification	Det Norske Veritas
IMO Number	9278234	MMSI Number	257182000
Length	223.75 m	Gross tonnage	75,027 GT
Beam	35.00 m	Net tonnage	48,197 NT
Draught	6.80 m	Deadweight	6,795 tdw
Passengers / Cabins	2,750 / 966	Maximum speed	22.1 kn
Vehicles	750 Cars	Cargo capacity	1,280 lm Lorries

Main engines	4 x Wärtsila W8L46B, Diesel / each 7,800 kW
Auxiliary engines	4 x Wärtsila 6L26A2, Diesel
Propeller	2 x 4-Blade Propeller, controllable pitch
Bow thruster	3 x Tunnel

Figure 33: M/S Color Magic   Photo: © SCANPIX NORGE/Terje Bendiksby

Name of ship	M/S Color Magic	

Home port / Flag state	Oslo / Norway	
Shipyard / Yard number	Aker Yards Oy, Turku, Finland / #1355	
Previous ship names	—	
Year of construction	2007	

Call sign	LNWC	Classification	Det Norske Veritas
IMO Number	9278234	**MMSI Number**	257182000
Length	223.75 m	**Gross tonnage**	75,156 GT
Beam	35.00 m	**Net tonnage**	47,529 NT
Draught	6.80 m	**Deadweight**	6,133 tdw
Passengers / Cabins	2,750 / 966	**Maximum speed**	22.1 kn
Vehicles	550 Cars	**Cargo capacity**	1,280 lm Lorries / Buses

Main engines	4 x 7,800 kW, Wärtsila W8L46B, Diesel / 31,200 kW
Auxiliary engines	4 x Wärtsila 6L26A2, Diesel
Propeller	2 x 4-Blade-Propeller, controllable pitch
Bow thruster	3 x Tunnel

Figure 34: M/S Color Viking   Photo: © Nordsveenfoto.no

Name of ship	M/S Color Viking	🏴

Home port / Flag state	Sandefjord / Norway
Shipyard / Yard number	A/S Nakskov Skipsvaerft, Nakskov, Denmark / #233
Previous ship names	1985-1991 Peder Paars, 1991-1998 Stena Invicta, 1998-2000 Wasa Jubilee
Year of construction	1985

Call sign	LLTF	Classification	Det Norske Veritas
IMO Number	8317942	MMSI Number	259278000
Length	137.00 m	Gross tonnage	19,763 GT
Beam	24.62 m	Net tonnage	6,076 NT
Draught	5.65 m	Deadweight	2,390 tdw
Passengers / Cabins	1,720 / 148	Maximum speed	18 kn
Vehicles	370 Cars	Cargo capacity	651 lm

Main engines	2 x MAN Burmeister & Wain 8L45GB, Diesel / 12,480 kW
Auxiliary engines	4 x MAN Burmeister & Wain 8S28 LU
Propeller	2 x Propeller, controllable pitch KaMeWa, Rolls-Royce AB
Bow thruster	2 x 2400B/AS-CP + 1 x Stern thruster 2400B/AS-CP

Figure 35: HSC SuperSpeed 1   Photo: © Kurt Engen

Name of ship — HSC SuperSpeed 1

Home port / Flag state	Kristiansand / Norway
Shipyard / Yard number	Aker Yards, Rauma, Finland / #1359
Previous ship names	—
Year of construction	2008

Call sign	JWNH	**Classification**	Det Norske Veritas
IMO Number	9374519	**MMSI Number**	259490000
Length	211.30 m	**Gross tonnage**	36,822 GT
Beam	26.00 m	**Net tonnage**	11,047 NT
Draught	6.70 m	**Deadweight**	5,400 tdw
Passengers / Cabins	2,315	**Maximum speed**	27 kn
Vehicles	750 Cars	**Cargo capacity**	1,990 lm

Main engines	4 x Wärtsilä 9L46, Diesel / each 9,600 kW
Auxiliary engines	4 x Wärtsilä 6L32, Diesel / each 3,000 kW
Propeller	2 x 4-Blade-Propeller, controllable pitch 150XF5/4
Bow thruster	3 x Tunnel (2 x Rolls-Royce TT 2650 AUX CP / 2,400 kW,
	1 x Rolls-Royce TT 2000 AUX CP / 1,200 kW)

Figure 36: HSC SuperSpeed 2   Photo: © Nordsveenfoto.no

Name of ship   HSC SuperSpeed 2   ╬

Home port / Flag state	Larvik / Norway
Shipyard / Yard number	Aker Yards, Rauma, Finland / #1360
Previous ship names	—
Year of construction	2008

Call sign	JWNE	Classification	Det Norske Veritas
IMO Number	9378682	MMSI Number	258092000
Length	211.30 m	Gross tonnage	34,231 GT
Beam	26.00 m	Net tonnage	10,269 NT
Draught	6.70 m	Deadweight	5,400 tdw
Passengers / Cabins	1929	Maximum speed	27 kn
Vehicles	764 Cars	Cargo capacity	2,036 lm

Main engines	4 x Wärtsilä 9L46, Diesel / each 9,600 kW
Auxiliary engines	4 x Wärtsilä 6L32, Diesel / each 3,000 kW
Propeller	2 x 4-Blade-Propeller, controllable pitch 150XF5/4
Bow thruster	3 x Tunnel (2 x Rolls-Royce TT 2650 AUX CP / 2,400 kW,
	1 x Rolls-Royce TT 2000 AUX CP / 1,200 kW)

Condor Ferries was founded in 1964 as a passenger ferry service between France and the Channel Islands. Since 1987 Condor Ferries connect with its RO/PAX ferries the Channel Islands all year round with the English ports Poole, Weymouth and Portsmouth. From Guernsey and from Jersey a regular ferry service to the French ports of St. Malo and Cherbourg was established. 1993 for Condor Ferries began the era of high-speed ferries with the commissioning of the Australian built InCat-catamaran ferry "Condor 10", travelling between the Channel Islands and the British port of Weymouth. On the "Condor 10" followed in 1995 the "Condor 11" and 1996 the "Condor 12", which were used each only one season and then they were sold. Later Condor acquired more InCat vessels: the "Condor Express", "Condor Vitesse" and "Condor Rapide". In 1999, Commodore Shipping took over Condor Ferries completely. The year 2002 brought a number of changes: the Commodore Group was sold to a management buy-out team for 150 million GBP. 2004, the Group was restructured and Commodore Ferries were integrated into Condor Ferries and Commodore Express renamed in Condor Logistics. In the same year Condor Ferries was sold to the Venture Capital Section of the Royal Bank of Scotland for 240 million GBP. 2008 Condor Ferries changed again of ownership. The new owner of the shipping company was the Australian Macquarie Group, who possess Condor Ferries until today. In 2015 Condor Ferries sold its "Condor Express" and the "Condor Vitesse" to the Greek ferry operator Seajets, now serving the Greek islands. In the same year Condor Ferries took over their new high speed ferry "Condor Liberation", changing at the same time also their corporate identity with a new, more modern company logo and a completely new internet presence. Besides its conventional ferries "Commodore Clipper" (passenger and freight) and "Commodore Goodwill" (only freight) currently Condor Ferries owns the two high speed ferries named "Condor Liberation" and "Condor Rapide". [13]

Figure 37: M/S Commodore Clipper   Photo: © Condor Ferries Ltd.

Name of ship   M/S Commodore Clipper

Home port / Flag state	Nassau / Bahamas
Shipyard / Yard number	Van der Giessen de Noord, Netherlands / #975
Previous ship names	—
Year of construction	1999

Call sign	C6QQ3	**Classification**	Det Norske Veritas
IMO Number	9201750	**MMSI Number**	308094000
Length	129.14 m	**Gross tonnage**	14,000 GT
Beam	23.40 m	**Net tonnage**	4,201 NT
Draught	5.80 m	**Deadweight**	4,504 tdw
Passengers / Cabins	500 / 40	**Maximum speed**	18.7 kn
Vehicles	279 Cars	**Cargo capacity**	1,265 lm

Main engines	2 x MAK 9M32, Diesel / 4,320 kW
Auxiliary engines	3 x Caterpillar 3508B DITA , Diesel
Propeller	2 x Propeller, controllable pitch
Bow thruster	2 x Tunnel

Figure 38: HSC Condor Liberation   Photo: © Condor Ferries Ltd.

Name of ship   HSC Condor Liberation

Home port / Flag state	Nassau / Bahamas
Shipyard / Yard number	Austal Ships Pty Ltd, Henderson, Australia / #270
Previous ship names	2010-2013 Austal 270, 2013-2014 Austal Hull 270, 2014-2015 Condor 102
Year of construction	2010

Call sign	C6YL4	Classification	Det Norske Veritas
IMO Number	9551363	MMSI Number	311037300
Length	102.00 m	Gross tonnage	6,307 GT
Beam	27.40 m	Net tonnage	1,892 NT
Draught	4.50 m	Deadweight	680 tdw
Passengers / Cabins	880 / No Cabins	Maximum speed	37 kn
Vehicles	245 Cars	Cargo capacity	188 lm

Main engines	3 x MTU 20V 8000 M71L, Diesel / 9,100 kW
Propeller	3 x Wärtsilä Lips LJX 1300 Waterjets

Figure 39: HSC Condor Rapide   Photo: © Condor Ferries Ltd.

Name of ship	HSC Condor Rapide	

Home port / Flag state   Nassau / Bahamas

Shipyard / Yard number   InCat Australia Pty.Ltd., Hobart, Australia / #045

Previous ship names   1997-1999 Incat 045, 1999-2001 HMAS Eachrvis Bay, 2001-2002 Eachrvis Bay, 2002-2004 Incat 045 , 2004-2004 Winner, 2004-2008 Speed One, 2009-2009 Sea Leopard

Year of construction   1997

Call sign	C6YK8	**Classification**	Det Norske Veritas
IMO Number	9161560	**MMSI Number**	311036800
Length	86.62 m	**Gross tonnage**	5,007 GT
Beam	26.00 m	**Net tonnage**	2,059 NT
Draught	3.628 m	**Deadweight**	415 tdw
Passengers / Cabins	900 / No Cabins	**Maximum speed**	48 kn
Vehicles	200 Cars	**Cargo capacity**	No Freight

Main engines   4 x Ruston 20RK270, Diesel / 28,320 kW

Auxiliary engines   4 x Caterpillar 3406 DITA, Diesel

Propeller   4 x Wärtsilä Lips LJ145D Waterjets

Figure 40: DFDS headquarter

Photo: © DFDS Seaways

DFDS has had a very eventful history. DFDS was born in 1866, as C.F.Tietgen merged the three largest Danish shipping companies at this time. From the beginning, DFDS carried both freight and Passengers in Denmark and outside the domestic market. The international ambitions of the DFDS included at the beginning the Baltic Sea and the North Sea, and a little later the Mediterranean region, the United States and South America. Based on a cruise ferry concept DFDS tried in 1982 to establish a route between New York and Miami, but had been buried these plans in 1983 due to lack of demand. Then the DFDS Group was restructured and as a result the activities in the Mediterranean and the routes to the USA and South America were sold. Since then DFDS has focused mainly on its activities in North Europe. Since then the shipping business of DFDS has grown steadily, particularly through the acquisition of the Lithuanian LISCO in 2001 and the Norwegian Lys-Line 2003. After 2007, a new management had taken over the company, DFDS also changed the strategic direction and took over in 2010 the Norfolkline from the Danish AP Moller–Maersk. With this move DFDS became the largest shipping and logistics company in northern Europe, with 25 routes and 55 ships. [14]

Transmanche Ferries is part of the DFDS freight and passenger ferry network, operating between the britsh port of Newhaven and the French Dieppe with two modern Ro-Pax ferries, the M/S "Côte d'Albâtre" and the M/S "Seven Sisters". Transmanche Ferries was formed after P&O Stena Line decided to concentrate the ferry traffic on the route Dover-Calais and to cancel the until 1998 existing ferry connection between Newhaven and Dieppe. [15]

Figure 41: M/S Athena Seaways   Photo: © DFDS Seaways

Name of ship   M/S Athena Seaways

Home port / Flag state	Klaipeda / Lithuania
Shipyard / Yard number	Nuovi Cantieri Apuania, Massa di Carrara, Italy / #1237
Previous ship names	2007-2013 M/S Coraggio
Year of construction	2007

Call sign	LYAC	**Classification**	Registro Navale Italiano
IMO Number	9350680	**MMSI Number**	277504000
Length	199.14 m	**Gross tonnage**	25,993 GT
Beam	26.60 m	**Net tonnage**	Unspecified
Draught	6.40 m	**Deadweight**	8,500 tdw
Passengers	600	**Maximum speed**	24 kn
Vehicles	Unspecified	**Cargo capacity**	2,490 lm

Main engines	2 x Wärtsilä 12V46, Diesel / each 12,600 kW
Auxiliary engines	4 x Diesel / 5,590 kW
Propeller	2 Propeller, controllable pitch
Bow thruster	2 x Tunnel

Figure 42: M/S Calais Seaways   Photo: © DFDS Seaways

Name of ship	M/S Calais Seaways	

Home port / Flag state	Le Havre / France
Shipyard / Yard number	Boelwerf Shipyard, Temse, Belgium / #1534
Previous ship names	1991-1998 Prins Filip, 1998-1999 Stena Royal, 1999-2002 POSL Aquitaine, 2002-2003 PO Aquitaine, 2003-2005 Pride of Aquitaine, 2005-2010 Norman Spirit, 2010-2011 Ostend Spirit, 2011-2013 Norman Spirit
Year of construction	1991

Call sign	FGXF	Classification	Bureau Veritas
IMO Number	8908466	**MMSI Number**	228006800
Length	163.61 m	**Gross tonnage**	28,833 GT
Beam	27.60 m	**Net tonnage**	11,596 NT
Draught	6.35 m	**Deadweight**	3,832 tdw
Passengers / Cabins	1,850 / 121	**Maximum speed**	21 kn
Vehicles	250 Cars	**Cargo capacity**	1,800 lm

Main engines	4 x Sulzer 8ZA S40, Diesel / each 5,280 kW
Auxiliary engines	4 x ABC Diesel / each 1,459 kW
Propeller	2 Propeller, controllable pitch, LB 10.00
Bow thruster	2 x Tunnel / 1,200 kW and 1 x 900 kW

Figure 43: M/S Côte d'Albâtre   Photo: © Philippe Alès / Wikimedia Commons CC-BY-SA-3.0

Name of ship	M/S Côte d'Albâtre

Home port / Flag state   Rouen / France

Shipyard / Yard number   Astilleros Hijos de J.Barreras S.A., Vigo, Spain / #1645

Previous ship names   -

Year of construction   2006

Call sign	FMHO	Classification	Bureau Veritas
IMO Number	9320128	MMSI Number	228233600
Length	142.63 m	Gross tonnage	18,425 GT
Beam	24.20 m	Net tonnage	5,527 NT
Draught	5.90 m	Deadweight	2,900 tdw
Passengers / Berths	600 / 196	Maximum speed	22 kn
Vehicles	224 Cars	Cargo capacity	1,270 lm

Main engines   2 x Wärtsilä 8L46C, Diesel / 18,900 kW

Auxiliary engines   3 x Diesel / 1,080 kW

Propeller   2 x Propeller, controllable pitch LB 10.00

Bow thruster   2 x Tunnel

Figure 44: M/S Côte des Dunes

Photo: © DFDS Seaways

Name of ship | M/S Côte des Dunes

Home port / Flag state	Le Havre / France
Shipyard / Yard number	Aker Finnyard Oy, Rauma, Finland / #437
Previous ship names	2001-2012 Seafrance Rodin, 2012-2016 Rodin
Year of construction	2001

Call sign	FOBQ	Classification	Bureau Veritas
IMO Number	9232527	MMSI Number	227022800
Length	185.82 m	Gross tonnage	33,796 GT
Beam	27.70 m	Net tonnage	11,502 NT
Draught	6.75 m	Deadweight	6,260 tdw
Passengers	1,900	Maximum speed	25 kn
Vehicles	714 Cars	Cargo capacity	2,000 lm or 120 Lorries

Main engines	2 x Wärtsilä 12V46B, Diesel / each 11,700 kW,
Auxiliary engines	2 x Wärtsilä 8L46B, Diesel / each 7,800 kW
Propeller	4 x Wärtsilä 8L20, Diesel / 1368 kW
Bow thruster	3 x Lips Bow thruster Tunnel, each 1,800 kW / 1 x Lips Stern thruster Tunnel / 1,800 kW

Figure 45: M/S Côte des Flandres   Photo: © DFDS Seaways

Name of ship	M/S Côte des Flandres

Home port / Flag state	Le Havre / France
Shipyard / Yard number	Chantiers de l'Atlantique, Saint Nazaire, France / #032
Previous ship names	2005-2012 Seafrance Berlioz, 2012-2016 Berlioz
Year of construction	2005

Call sign	FMAB	Classification	Bureau Veritas
IMO Number	9305843	**MMSI Number**	228085000
Length	185,82 m	**Gross tonnage**	33,796 GT
Beam	27.70 m	**Net tonnage**	11,502 NT
Draught	6.75 m	**Deadweight**	6,260 tdw
Passengers	1,900	**Maximum speed**	25 kn
Vehicles	714 Cars	**Cargo capacity**	2,000 lm or 120 Lorries

Main engines	2 x Wärtsilä 12V46B, Diesel / each 11,700 kW, 2 x Wärtsilä 8L46B, Diesel / each 7,800 kW
Auxiliary engines	4 x Diesel / 1,368 kW
Propeller	2 x Propeller, controllable pitch Lips LB 10.00
Bow thruster	3 x Lips Bow thruster Tunnel, each 1,800 kW / 1 x Lips Stern thruster Tunnel / 1,800 kW

Figure 46: M/S Crown Seaways

Photo: © DFDS Seaways

Name of ship	M/S Crown Seaways	

Home port / Flag state	Copenhagen / Denmark
Shipyard / Yard number	Brodosplit brodogradilište d.o.o, Split, Croatia / #373
Previous ship names	1994-2013 Crown of Scandinavia
Year of construction	1994

Call sign	OXRA6	**Classification**	Det Norske Veritas
IMO Number	8917613	**MMSI Number**	219592000
Length	171.00 m	**Gross tonnage**	35,498 GT
Beam	28.20 m	**Net tonnage**	21,021 NT
Draught	6.368 m	**Deadweight**	2,940 tdw
Passengers	2,136	**Maximum speed**	21.5 kn
Vehicles	450 Cars	**Cargo capacity**	970 lm

Main engines	4 x Pielstick 12PC2-6/2V, Diesel / 23,760 kW
Auxiliary engines	4 x Wärtsilä 6R32BC, Diesel
Propeller	2 x Propeller, controllable pitch KaMeWa 157XF3/4
Bow thruster	2 x KaMeWa 2400 D/AS CP, Tunnel

Figure 47: M/S Delft Seaways   Photo: © DFDS Seaways

Name of ship — M/S Delft Seaways

Home port / Flag state	Dover / United Kingdom
Shipyard / Yard number	Samsung Heavy Industries, Geoje, South Korea / #1524
Previous ship names	2006-2010 Maersk Delft
Year of construction	2006

Call sign	MJYC9	Classification	Lloyd's Register of Shipping
IMO Number	9293088	MMSI Number	235009590
Length	186.65 m	Gross tonnage	34,500 GT
Beam	28.40 m	Net tonnage	10,300 NT
Draught	6.75 m	Deadweight	6,160 tdw
Passengers	780	Maximum speed	25 kn
Vehicles	200 Cars	Cargo capacity	1,800 lm or 120 Lorries

Main engines	4 x MAN B&W 8L48/60B, Diesel / 38,400 kW
Auxiliary engines	Unspecified
Propeller	2 x Propeller, controllable pitch
Bow thruster	3 x Tunnel

Figure 48: M/S Dover Seaways · Photo: © DFDS Seaways

Name of ship — M/S Dover Seaways

Home port / Flag state   Dover / United Kingdom

Shipyard / Yard number   Samsung Heavy Industries, Geoje, South Korea / #1574

Previous ship names   2006-2010 Maersk Dover

Year of construction   2006

Call sign	MLBZ6	Classification	Lloyd´s Register of Shipping
IMO Number	9318345	MMSI Number	235010500
Length	186.00 m	Gross tonnage	35,923 GT
Beam	28.00 m	Net tonnage	10,300 NT
Draught	6.20 m	Deadweight	6,874 tdw
Passengers / Cabins	780 / 9	Max. speed	25 kn
Vehicles	200 Cars	Cargo capacity	1,800 lm or 120 Lorries

Main engines   4 x MAN 8L48/60B, Diesel / 38,400 kW

Auxiliary engines   Unspecified

Propeller   2 x Propeller, controllable pitch

Bow thruster   3 x Tunnel

Figure 49: M/S Dunkerque Seaways   Photo: © DFDS Seaways

Name of ship   M/S Dunkerque Seaways

Home port / Flag state	Dover / United Kingdom
Shipyard / Yard number	Samsung Heavy Industries, Geoje, South Korea / #1523
Previous ship names	2005-2010 Maersk Dunkerque
Year of construction	2005

Call sign	MJTL2	Classification	Lloyd´s Register of Shipping
IMO Number	9293076	**MMSI Number**	235028825
Length	189.00 m	**Gross tonnage**	35,923 GT
Beam	28.40 m	**Net tonnage**	10,776 NT
Draught	5.80 m	**Deadweight**	6,787 tdw
Passengers	780	**Max. speed**	25 kn
Vehicles	200 Cars	**Cargo capacity**	1,800 lm or 120 Lorries

Main engines	4 x MAN 8L48/ 60B, Diesel / 38,400 kW
Auxiliary engines	Unspecified
Propeller	2 x Propeller, controllable pitch
Bow thruster	2 x Tunnel

Figure 50: M/S King Seaways   Photo: © DFDS Seaways

Name of ship — M/S King Seaways

Home port / Flag state	Copenhagen / Denmark
Shipyard / Yard number	Schichau Seebeckwerft, Bremerhaven, Germany / #1059
Previous ship names	1992-1993 Nils Holgersson, 1993-2006 Val de Loire, 2006-2011 King of Scandinavia
Year of construction	1995

Call sign	OVOL2	Classification	Bureau Veritas
IMO Number	8502406	MMSI Number	220449000
Length	162.73 m	Gross tonnage	31,395 GT
Beam	27.60 m	Net tonnage	13,212 NT
Draught	6.50 m	Deadweight	4,110 tdw
Passengers / Cabins	2,280 / 505	Maximum speed	21.3 kn
Vehicles	570 Cars	Cargo capacity	1,250 lm

Main engines	4 x MAK, Diesel / 19,600 kW
Auxiliary engines	5 x Diesel / each 1,536 kW
Propeller	2 x Propeller, controllable pitch LB 10.00
Bow thruster	2 x Tunnel

Figure 51: M/S Liverpool Seaways   Photo: © DFDS Seaways

Name of ship	M/S Liverpool Seaways

Home port / Flag state	Klaipeda / Lithuania
Shipyard / Yard number	Cantieri Navale Visentini, Donada, Italy / #182
Previous ship names	1997-2005 Lagan Viking, 2005-2010 Liverpool Viking
Year of construction	1997

Call sign	LYTK	**Classification**	Det Norske Veritas
IMO Number	9136034	**MMSI Number**	277449000
Length	186.00 m	**Gross tonnage**	21,856 GT
Beam	26.00 m	**Net tonnage**	6,580 NT
Draught	5.55 m	**Deadweight**	7,115 tdw
Passengers / Cabins	340 / 72	**Maximum speed**	21.5 kn
Vehicles	200 Cars	**Cargo capacity**	2,460 lm

Main engines	2 x Wärtsilä 8R46 LNE, Diesel / 15,600 kW
Auxiliary engines	3 x Caterpillar 3512 / each 1,070 kW
Propeller	2 x Propeller, controllable pitch Wärtsilä / Wichman PR 108/4H
Bow thruster	2 x Berg Propulsion SP8 + 1 x Rolls-Royce TT1850CP

Figure 52: M/S Optima Seaways   Photo: © DFDS Seaways

Name of ship	M/S Optima Seaways

Home port / Flag state	Klaipeda / Lithuania
Shipyard / Yard number	Cantiere Navale Visentini, Donada, Italy / #1166
Previous ship names	1999-2001 Alyssa, 2001-2006 Svealand, 2006-2012 Lisco Optima
Year of construction	1999

Call sign	LYSD	Classification	Lloyd's Register of Shipping
IMO Number	9188427	**MMSI Number**	277339000
Length	186.00 m	**Gross tonnage**	25,206 GT
Beam	25.60 m	**Net tonnage**	7,744 NT
Draught	6.50 m	**Deadweight**	7,500 tdw
Passengers	328	**Max. speed**	21.5 kn
Vehicles	135 Cars	**Cargo capacity**	2,240 lm

Main engines	2 x MAN/B&W type 9L 48/60, Diesel / each 9,450 kW
Auxiliary engines	Unspecified
Propeller	2 x Propeller, controllable pitch
Bow thruster	2 x Tunnel

Figure 53: M/S Patria Seaways   Photo: © Johan Fredriksson/Wiki Commons CC-BY-3.0

Name of ship	M/S Patria Seaways

Home port / Flag state	Klaipeda / Lithuania
Shipyard / Yard number	Fosen Mekaniske Verksteder A/S, Rissa, Norway / #51
Previous ship names	1991-1992, 1995-1997, 2002-2004 Stena Traveller, 1992-1995, 1997-2002 TT-Traveller,2004-2011 Lisco Patria
Year of construction	1991

Call sign	LYRC	Classification	American Bureau of Shipping
IMO Number	8917390	**MMSI Number**	277291000
Length	154.00 m	**Gross tonnage**	18,332 GT
Beam	24.33 m	**Net tonnage**	5,499 NT
Draught	5.90 m	**Deadweight**	4,758 tdw
Passengers / Cabins	243 / 204	**Maximum speed**	18 kn
Vehicles	480 Cars	**Cargo capacity**	1,710 lm

Main engines	2 x Wärtsilä Sulzer 8ZA40S, Diesel / each 5,280 kW
Auxiliary engines	3 x Diesel, each 560 kW
Propeller	2 x Propeller, controllable pitch
Bow thruster	2 x Tunnel

Figure 54: M/S Pearl Seaways

Photo: © DFDS Seaways

Name of ship	M/S Pearl Seaways	

Home port / Flag state	Copenhagen / Denmark
Shipyard / Yard number	Wärtsilä Turku Shipyard, Turku, Finland / #1297
Previous ship names	1989-1993 Athena, 1993-1993 Star Aquarius, 1993-2001 Langkapuri Star Aqua, 2001-2001 Aquarius, 2001-2010 Pearl of Scandinavia
Year of construction	1989

Call sign	OWFU2	**Classification**	Det Norske Veritas
IMO Number	8701674	**MMSI Number**	219945000
Length	178.40 m	**Gross tonnage**	40,039 GT
Beam	29.61 m	**Net tonnage**	23,052 NT
Draught	6.215 m	**Deadweight**	2,800 tdw
Passengers / Cabins	2,200 / 704	**Maximum speed**	21 kn
Vehicles	350 Cars	**Cargo capacity**	1,008 lm

Main engines	4 x Wärtsilä-Sulzer 9ZAL40S, Diesel / 23,760 kW
Auxiliary engines	4 x Wärtsilä 6R32D, Diesel
Propeller	2 x Propeller, controllable pitch KaMeWa 2X157XF3/4
Bow thruster	2 x KaMeWa 2400 D/AS-CP, Tunnel

Figure 55: M/S Princess Seaways

Photo: © DFDS Seaways

Name of ship	M/S Princess Seaways ╬

Home port / Flag state	Copenhagen / Denmark
Shipyard / Yard number	Schichau Seebeckwerft, Bremerhaven, Germany/ #1058
Previous ship names	1986-1993 Peter Pan, 1993-2002 Spirit of Tasmania, 2002-2003 Spir, 2003-2006 Fjord Norway, 2006-2011 Princess of Norway
Year of construction	1986

Call sign	OXED2	Classification	Det Norske Veritas
IMO Number	8502391	**MMSI Number**	220489000
Length	161.53 m	**Gross tonnage**	31,356 GT
Beam	28.20 m	**Net tonnage**	14,025 NT
Draught	6.217 m	**Deadweight**	4,110 tdw
Passengers / Cabins	1,460 / 469	**Maximum speed**	18.5 kn
Vehicles	Unspecified	**Cargo capacity**	Unspecified

Main engines	4 x MAK 8M552, Diesel / 19,600 kW
Auxiliary engines	4 x Sulzer 9L28/32, Diesel
Propeller	2 x Propeller, controllable pitch Escher Wyss 400GAP
Bow thruster	2 x Brunvoll FU100LTC2450, Tunnel

Figure 56: M/S Regina Seaways

Photo: © DFDS Seaways

Name of ship	M/S Regina Seaways	

Home port / Flag state	Klaipeda / Lithuania
Shipyard / Yard number	Nuovi Cantieri Apuania, Massa Carrara, Italy / #1244
Previous ship names	2010-2011 Energia
Year of construction	2010

Call sign	LYTO	Classification	Registro Italiano Navale
IMO Number	9458535	MMSI Number	277466000
Length	176.92 m	Gross tonnage	25,518 GT
Beam	26.60 m	Net tonnage	Unspecified
Draught	6.40 m	Deadweight	7,500 tdw
Passengers / Cabins	600	Maximum speed	24 kn
Vehicles	600 Cars	Cargo capacity	2,623 lm

Main engines	2 x Wärtsilä 12V46, Diesel / 24,000 kW
Auxiliary engines	Unspecified
Propeller	2 x Propeller, controllable pitch
Bow thruster	2 x Tunnel

Figure 57: M/S Seven Sisters

Photo: © Alf van Beem / Wikimedia Commons CC-0-1.0

Name of ship	M/S Seven Sisters

Home port / Flag state	Dieppe / France
Shipyard / Yard number	Astilleros Hijos de J.Barreras S.A., Vigo, Spain / #1646
Previous ship names	-
Year of construction	2006

Call sign	FMJR	Classification	Bureau Veritas
IMO Number	9320130	MMSI Number	228244700
Length	142.63 m	Gross tonnage	18,425 GT
Beam	24.20 m	Net tonnage	5,527 NT
Draught	5.90 m	Deadweight	2,900 tdw
Passengers / Cabins	600 / 196	Maximum speed	22 kn
Vehicles	224 Cars	Cargo capacity	1,270 lm

Main engines	2 x Wärtsilä 8L46C, Diesel / 18,900 kW
Auxiliary engines	3 x Diesel / 1,080 kW
Propeller	2 x Propeller, controllable pitch LB 10.00
Bow thruster	2 x Tunnel

Figure 58: M/S Victoria Seaways

Name of ship	M/S Victoria Seaways

Home port / Flag state	Klaipeda / Lithuania
Shipyard / Yard number	Nuovi Cantieri Apuania, Massa Carrara, Italy / #1241
Previous ship names	2008-2012 Lisco Maxima
Year of construction	2008

Call sign	LYTD	Classification	Registro Italiano Navale
IMO Number	9350721	MMSI Number	277408000
Length	176.92 m	Gross tonnage	25,518 GT
Beam	26.60 m	Net tonnage	11,568 NT
Draught	5.50 m	Deadweight	7,000 tdw
Passengers / Cabins	515	Maximum speed	23.5 kn
Vehicles	600 Cars	Cargo capacity	2,630 lm

Main engines	2 x Wärtsilä 12V46C, Diesel / 24,000 kW
Auxiliary engines	3 x Diesel / 5,040 kW
Propeller	2 x Propeller, controllable pitch
Bow thruster	2 x Tunnel

Figure 59: M/S Vilnius Seaways   Photo: © DFDS Seaways

Name of ship — M/S Vilnius Seaways

Home port / Flag state	Klaipeda / Lithuania
Shipyard / Yard number	Matthias-Thesen-Werft, Wismar, Germany / #323
Previous ship names	1987-2011 Vilnius
Year of construction	1987

Call sign	LYAI	**Classification**	Lloyd's Register of Shipping
IMO Number	8311900	**MMSI Number**	277093000
Length	190.93 m	**Gross tonnage**	22,341 GT
Beam	26.01 m	**Net tonnage**	6,702 NT
Draught	6.50 m	**Deadweight**	9,341 tdw
Passengers	132	**Maximum speed**	16 kn
Vehicles	Unspecified	**Cargo capacity**	1,700 lm

Main engines	4 x 6VDS 48/42 AL-2, Diesel / 10,600 kW
Auxiliary engines	Unspecified
Propeller	2 Propeller, controllable pitch
Bow thruster	2 x Tunnel / each 740 kW

Rederiaktiebolaget Eckerö was founded on March 2, 1961 and is the parent company of Eckerö Group, which consists of the following five divisions:
Eckerö Linjen - Ro-Pax ferry traffic between Eckerö (Åland) and Grisslehamn (Sweden)
Eckerö Line - Ro-Pax ferry traffic between Helsinki (Finland) and Tallinn (Estonia)
Birka Cruises - Passenger traffic between Stockholm (Sweden) and Mariehamn (Åland)
Eckerö Shipping Ab Ltd - Ro Ro - Cargo Traffic (worldwide, but mainly Europe)
Williams Buss - bus service on the Åland islands and distance coaches
As for the ferry traffic on the Baltic and the North Sea only Eckerö Linjen and Eckerö Line are relevant to the scope of this book, we consider only these two lines of business of the Group Eckerö. [16]

ECKERÖ⊜LINJEN

Eckerö Linjen is a Finnish ferry company, based on the Åland Islands, which belongs to the Rederiaktiebolaget Eckerö group. Other business divisions of Eckerö Linjen are the travel agency brands Ålandsresor and Ålandsresor Resebyrå which are selling the group's own ferry connections, cruises and bus trips as well as various third-party products such as flight bookings, hotel accommodations, travel packages etc.

Eckerö Linjen began with the regular ferry service in 1961 between Eckerö (Åland) and Grisslehamn (Sweden) with relatively small ferries. As a first bigger ferry unit in 1982 the "M/S Eckerö" was commissioned and since 2005 the much larger M/S "Jens Kofoed", bought from Bornholmstrafikken, took over the ferry service on the route Eckerö-Grisslehamn, now renamed "M/S Eckerö". Even if Eckerö Linjen and Eckerö Line are legally two different companies, the ships of one company sometimes are used when needed for the other line. [17]

ECKERÖ⊜LINE

Eckerö Line was founded in 1994, is part of the Eckerö Group and based in Mariehamn on the Åland Islands belonging to Finland. Eckerö Line operates the route between the Estonian capital Tallinn and the Finnish capital Helsinki. [18]

Figure 60: M/S Eckerö   Photo: © Eckerö Linjen

Name of ship	M/S Eckerö	

Home port / Flag state	Grisslehamn / Sweden
Shipyard / Yard number	Aalborg Vaerft A/S, Aalborg, Denmark / #222
Previous ship names	1979-2005 Jens Kofoed
Year of construction	1979

Call sign	SBJU	Classification	Bureau Veritas
IMO Number	7633155	MMSI Number	266308000
Length	121.10 m	Gross tonnage	12,358 GT
Beam	21.50 m	Net tonnage	4,376 NT
Draught	5.25 m	Deadweight	1,940 tdw
Passengers / Berths	1,630 / 481	Maximum speed	20.5 kn
Vehicles	265 Cars	Cargo capacity	515 lm

Main engines	4 x B&W-Alpha 16U28LU-VO, Diesel / 12.241 kW
Auxiliary engines	1 x Diesel / 745 kW + 2 x Diesel / 860 kW
Propeller	2 x Propeller, controllable pitch 10.00
Bow thruster	2 x Tunnel

Figure 61: M/S Finlandia
Photo: © Eckerö Line

Name of ship   M/S Finlandia

Home port / Flag state	Eckerö / Finland
Shipyard / Yard number	Daewoo Shipbuilding & Heavy Machinery Ltd., Okpo, South Korea / #7506
Previous ship names	2001-2012 Moby Freedom, 2012-2012 Freedom
Year of construction	2001

Call sign	OJPP	Classification	Bureau Veritas
IMO Number	9214379	**MMSI Number**	230628000
Length	174.99 m	**Gross tonnage**	36,365 GT
Beam	27.60 m	**Net tonnage**	15,434 NT
Draught	7.00 m	**Deadweight**	5,506 tdw
Passengers / Berths	2,080 / 1,190	**Maximum speed**	27 kn
Vehicles	655 Cars	**Cargo capacity**	1,950 lm

Main engines	4 x Wärtsilä 12V46, Diesel / 50,400 kW
Auxiliary engines	4 x Diesel / 1,408 kW
Propeller	2 x Propeller, controllable pitch 10.00
Bow thruster	2 x Tunnel

Figure 62 M/S Langeland in sunset   Photo: © Danske Færger A/S

Danske Færger A/S (Denmark)

Færgen can look back on a long history rich in tradition as one of the oldest Danish ferry lines. The origin of the ferry line Færgen goes back to the year 1866. This year, the "Dampskibsselskabet på Bornholm af 1866" (Steamship company on Bornholm from 1866) was founded. After taking over the responsibility for the ferry connection to Bornholm in 1973, the shipping company was renamed "Bornholmstrafikken". On April 16, 2007 Clipper Group A/S and Bornholmstrafikken A/S formed the "Nordic Ferry Services (NFS)", based on Bornholm. After Clipper Invest in November 2007 took over "Sydfynske A/S" from "Scandlines", it was decided on January 14, 2011 to merge Bornholmstrafikken A/S, Sydfynske A/S and Nordic Ferry Services A/S. A new company was born, the "Danske Færger A/S", in everyday parlance named "Færgen". [19] Today Danske Færger A/S is divided into the regional ferry services:

Als Færgen
Bornholmer Færgen
Fanø Færgen
Langelands Færgen
Samsø Færgen

Figure 63: M/S Fenja

Photo: © FanøFærgen

Name of ship — M/S Fenja

Home port / Flag state	Esbjerg / Denmark
Shipyard / Yard number	Morsø Værft A/S, Nykøbing Mors, Denmark / #202
Previous ship names	-
Year of construction	1998

Call sign	OYIQ	Classification	Lloyd's Register of Shipping
IMO Number	9189378	MMSI Number	219000604
Length	49.90 m	Gross tonnage	751 GT
Beam	13.40 m	Net tonnage	274 NT
Draught	2.30 m	Deadweight	250 tdw
Passengers	395 (Summer) or 296 (Winter)	Maximum speed	11.5 kn
Vehicles	35 Cars	Cargo capacity	80 lm

Main engines	2 x Caterpillar 3412-E, Diesel / 1,618 kW
Auxiliary engines	Unspecified
Propeller	1 Azimuth Propeller Bow and 1 Azimuth Prop. Stern
Bow thruster	Function taken over by Azimuth Propellers

Figure 64: M/S Frigg Sydfyen

Photo: © Als Færgen

Name of ship | M/S Frigg Sydfyen

Home port / Flag state Spodsbjerg / Denmark

Shipyard / Yard number Svendborg Skibsværft A/S, Svendborg, Denmark / #172

Previous ship names -

Year of construction 1984

Call sign	OWNM	Classification	Lloyd´s Register of Shipping
IMO Number	8222824	MMSI Number	219000606
Length	70.01 m	Gross tonnage	1,676 GT
Beam	12.01 m	Net tonnage	826 NT
Draught	3.25 m	Deadweight	459 tdw
Passengers	338 (Summer) or 200 (Winter)	Maximum speed	13.5 kn
Vehicles	50 Cars	Cargo capacity	160 lm

Main engines 2 x MAN B&W Alpha 6T23L-KVO, Diesel / each 685 kW

Auxiliary engines 4 x Scania, Diesel

Propeller 2 x Propeller, controllable pitch

Bow thruster 2 x Tunnel

Figure 65: M/S Hammerodde

Photo: © Bornholmer Færgen

Name of ship	M/S Hammerodde	

Home port / Flag state	Rønne / Denmark
Shipyard / Yard number	IHC Merwede BV, Hardinxveld-Giessendam, Netherlands / #702
Previous ship names	-
Year of construction	2005

Call sign	OYAX	Classification	Bureau Veritas
IMO Number	9323699	MMSI Number	220378000
Length	129.90 m	Gross tonnage	14,551 GT
Beam	23.40 m	Net tonnage	5,157 NT
Draught	5.60 m	Deadweight	5,142 tdw
Passengers / Berths	400 / 168	Maximum speed	18.5 kn
Vehicles	200 Cars	Cargo capacity	1,500 lm

Main engines	2 x MAK 9M32, Diesel / 8,640 kW
Auxiliary engines	3 x MAN B&W, Diesel / 1,545 kW
Propeller	2 x Propeller, controllable pitch
Bow thruster	2 x Tunnel

Figure 66: M/S Kanhave   Photo: © Samsø Færgen

Name of ship   M/S Kanhave   ✚

Home port / Flag state	Sælvig / Denmark
Shipyard / Yard number	G Fratzis Shipyards, Perama, Greece / #P87
Previous ship names	-
Year of construction	2009

Call sign	OYHS	**Classification**	Bureau Veritas
IMO Number	9548562	**MMSI Number**	220619000
Length	91.43 m	**Gross tonnage**	4,630 GT
Beam	16.20 m	**Net tonnage**	1,389 NT
Draught	3.00 m	**Deadweight**	778 tdw
Passengers	600 (including Crew)	**Maximum speed**	16 kn
Vehicles	90 Cars	**Cargo capacity**	No Freight

Main engines	4 x Mitsubishi S16 MTPA, Diesel / 4,680 kW
Auxiliary engines	2 x Diesel / 312 kW
Propeller	4 x Azimuth Propeller Solid 5.00
Bow thruster	Unspecified

Figure 67: M/S Kyholm   Photo: © Samsø Færgen

Name of ship — M/S Kyholm

Home port / Flag state	Kolby Kås / Denmark
Shipyard / Yard number	Orskov Yard, Frederikshavn, Denmark / #205
Previous ship names	-
Year of construction	1998

Call sign	OZPH	Classification	Bureau Veritas
IMO Number	9183025	**MMSI Number**	219000577
Length	69.20 m	**Gross tonnage**	3,380 GT
Beam	14.80 m	**Net tonnage**	1,014 NT
Draught	3.20 m	**Deadweight**	489 tdw
Passengers	550 (Summer) or 390 (Winter)	**Maximum speed**	14.8 kn
Vehicles	90 Cars	**Cargo capacity**	9 Lorries

Main engines	2 x MAN B&W Alpha 6L28/32A-DVO, Diesel / 2,866 kW
Auxiliary engines	3 x Diesel / 189 kW
Propeller	2 x Propeller
Bow thruster	2 x Tunnel

Figure 68: M/S Langeland   Photo: © Langelands Færgen

Name of ship   M/S Langeland   +

Home port / Flag state   Spodsbjerg / Denmark

Shipyard / Yard number   J. J. Sietas Schiffswerft GmbH&Co.KG , Hamburg, Germany / #1296

Previous ship names   -

Year of construction   2012

Call sign	OZCU	Classification	Lloyd´s Register of Shipping
IMO Number	9596428	MMSI Number	219016938
Length	99.90 m	Gross tonnage	4,500 GT
Beam	18.20 m	Net tonnage	1,350 NT
Draught	3.00 m	Deadweight	949 tdw
Passengers	600 (Summer) or 450 (Winter)	Maximum speed	16 kn
Vehicles	122 Cars	Cargo capacity	No Freight

Main engines   5 x Caterpilar C32, Diesel / 3,496 kW

Auxiliary engines   Unspecified

Propeller   4 x Schottel Propeller

Figure 69: HSC Leonora Christina

Photo: © Bornholmer Færgen

Name of ship	HSC Leonora Christina	

Home port / Flag state	Rønne / Denmark
Shipyard / Yard number	Austal Ships Pty Ltd, Henderson, Australia / #246
Previous ship names	-
Year of construction	2011

Call sign	OWGM2	**Classification**	Det Norske Veritas
IMO Number	9557848	**MMSI Number**	219282000
Length	112.60 m	**Gross tonnage**	10,371 GT
Beam	27.50 m	**Net tonnage**	3,112 NT
Draught	3.80 m	**Deadweight**	1,000 tdw
Passengers	1,400	**Maximum speed**	40 kn
Vehicles	359 Cars	**Cargo capacity**	No Freight

Main engines	4 x MAN B&W 20V 28/33D, Diesel / each 9,100 kW
Auxiliary engines	4 x Volvo Penta, Diesel
Propeller	4 x Waterjet Rolls-Royce KaMeWa 125 S3NP
Bow thruster	2 (retractable)

Figure 70: M/S Lolland

Photo: © Langelands Færgen

Name of ship   M/S Lolland

Home port / Flag state	Sælvig / Denmark
Shipyard / Yard number	J. J. Sietas Schiffswerft GmbH & Co.KG , Hamburg, Germany / #1295
Previous ship names	2011-2012 Samsø
Year of construction	2011

Call sign	OYRK	Classification	Lloyd´s Register of Shipping
IMO Number	9594690	MMSI Number	219016555
Length	99.90 m	Gross tonnage	4,500 GT
Beam	18.20 m	Net tonnage	1,350 NT
Draught	3.00 m	Deadweight	949 tdw
Passengers	600 (Summer) or 450 (Winter)	Maximum speed	16 kn
Vehicles	122 Cars	Cargo capacity	No Freight

Main engines	5 x Caterpilar C32, Diesel / 3,496 kW
Auxiliary engines	Unspecified
Propeller	4 x Schottel Propeller

Figure 71: M/S Menja   Photo: © FanøFærgen

Name of ship   M/S Menja

Home port / Flag state	Esbjerg / Denmark
Shipyard / Yard number	Morsø Værft A/S, Nykøbing Mors, Denmark / #202
Previous ship names	-
Year of construction	1998

Call sign	OYIU	Classification	Lloyd's Register of Shipping
IMO Number	9189380	MMSI Number	219000603
Length	49.90 m	Gross tonnage	751 GT
Beam	13.40 m	Net tonnage	274 NT
Draught	2.30 m	Deadweight	250 tdw
Passengers	395 (Summer) or 296 (Winter)	Maximum speed	11.5 kn
Vehicles	35 Cars	Cargo capacity	80 lm

Main engines	2 x Caterpillar 3412-E, Diesel / 1,618 kW
Auxiliary engines	Unspecified
Propeller	1 Azimuth Propeller Bow and 1 Azimuth Prop. Stern
Bow thruster	Function taken over by Azimuth Propellers

Figure 72: M/S Odin Sydfyen

Photo: © Als Færgen

Name of ship — M/S Odin Sydfyen 🇩🇰

Home port / Flag state	Tårs / Denmark
Shipyard / Yard number	Svendborg Skibsværft A/S, Svendborg, Denmark / #168
Previous ship names	-
Year of construction	1982

Call sign	OURL	**Classification**	Lloyd´s Register of Shipping
IMO Number	8027896	**MMSI Number**	219000607
Length	70.32 m	**Gross tonnage**	1,698 GT
Beam	12.03 m	**Net tonnage**	509 NT
Draught	3.25 m	**Deadweight**	450 tdw
Passengers / Cabins	338 (Summer) or 200 (Winter)	**Maximum speed**	13.5 kn
Vehicles	55 Cars	**Cargo capacity**	140 lm

Main engines	2 x MAN B&W Alpha 6T23L-KVO, Diesel / each 685 kW
Auxiliary engines	4 x Scania, Diesel
Propeller	2 x Propeller, controllable pitch
Bow thruster	2 x Tunnel

Figure 73: M/S Povl Anker   Photo: © Bornholmer Færgen

Name of ship	M/S Povl Anker	

Home port / Flag state	Rønne / Denmark
Shipyard / Yard number	Danyard-Aalborg A/S, Aalborg, Denmark / #0221
Previous ship names	-
Year of construction	1978

Call sign	OYRA2	**Classification**	Bureau Veritas
IMO Number	7633143	**MMSI Number**	219173000
Length	121.10 m	**Gross tonnage**	12,358 GT
Beam	21.50 m	**Net tonnage**	4,376 NT
Draught	5.25 m	**Deadweight**	1,940 tdw
Passengers / Berths	1,500 / 490	**Maximum speed**	20.5 kn
Vehicles	262 Cars	**Cargo capacity**	515 lm or 26 Lorries

Main engines	4 x B&W-Alpha-Diesel / each 2,294 kW
Auxiliary engines	4 x Diesel / 574 kW
Propeller	2 x Propeller, controllable pitch LB 10.00
Bow thruster	2 x Tunnel

Figure 74: M/S Sønderho   Photo: © EHRENBERG Kommunikation/ Wiki Commons CC BY-SA 2.0

Name of ship	M/S Sønderho	

Home port / Flag state	Esbjerg / Denmark
Shipyard / Yard number	Esbjerg Jernstoberi & Maskinfabrik, Esbjerg, Denmark / #2
Previous ship names	-
Year of construction	1962

Call sign	OYVH	**Classification**	Lloyd's Register of Shipping
IMO Number	8946779	**MMSI Number**	219000605
Length	26.30 m	**Gross tonnage**	93 GT
Beam	6.10 m	**Net tonnage**	53 NT
Draught	1.21 m	**Deadweight**	21 tdw
Passengers	199	**Maximum speed**	10 kn
Vehicles	No Vehicles	**Cargo capacity**	No Freight

Main engines	1 x Scania DSI 1140 A22S, Diesel / 235 kW
Auxiliary engines	1 Valmet, Diesel / 40 kW
Propeller	1 x Propeller, controllable pitch
Bow thruster	1 x Tunnel

Figure 75: HSC Villum Clausen   Photo: © Bornholmer Færgen

Name of ship	HSC Villum Clausen

Home port / Flag state   Rønne / Denmark

Shipyard / Yard number   Austal Ships Pty Ltd, Henderson, Australia / #96

Previous ship names   -

Year of construction   2000

Call sign	OYVY2	Classification	Bureau Veritas
IMO Number	9216250	MMSI Number	219653000
Length	86.60 m	Gross tonnage	6,402 BRT
Beam	24.00 m	Net tonnage	1,921 NRT
Draught	4.03 m	Deadweight	485 tdw
Passengers	1,055	Maximum speed	49.5 kn
Vehicles	215 Cars or 10 Buses + 144 Cars	Cargo capacity	No Freight

Main engines   2 x Gas turbines General Electric GE LM 2500 / each 18,000 kW

Auxiliary engines   4 x Volvo Penta, Diesel / each 224 kW

Propeller   4 x Waterjet 5.00

Bow thruster   2 (retractable)

Finnlines is part of the Italian shipping company Grimaldi Group and is one of the largest RO/RO and RO/PAX shipping companies in Northern Europe. Finnlines focus its activities on the Baltic Sea traffic between Germany, Finland, Sweden and Russia. Except under the name Finnlines the shipping company operates under the name FinnLink on the route between Naantali and Kapellskar, under the name NordöLink between Travemünde and Malmö as well as with the designation TransRussiaExpress between Lübeck and St. Petersburg. Also part of Finnlines is the port operating company Finnsteve for freight service in the Finnish ports of Helsinki, Turku and Kotka. [20]

The history of Finnlines already goes back to the year 1947, when the shipping company was founded under the name "Oy Finn Lines Ltd." for the regular transportation of pulp and paper from Finland to the USA. In 1948 another shipping company saw the daylight - the "Finland Steamship Co.Ltd.", which was also in service on the routes from Finland to the United States and to Canada. Between the two companies was developed a close cooperation, which led to the establishment of the joint marketing venture "Oy Finncarriers Ab" in 1975. Each of the two companies held a 50% stake. Finncarriers worked for many years together with the Lübeck based "Poseidon Marine AG", before in 1998 the "Poseidon Schiffahrt" through a share swap has been incorporated into the Finn Lines Group. In the course of further expansion, the Swedish "NordöLink AB" was taken over in 2003, which has been travelling in the cargo traffic between Malmö and Travemünde. In 2009 NordöLink transformed from a pure freight shipping company in a mixed freight / passenger shipping company. Using the synergy effects with the Grimaldi Group, which owns the majority of Finnlines since 2006, cargo can be transported to Southern Europe, North Africa and America. [21]

Figure 76: Loading in the port   Graphic: © Finnlines

Figure 77: M/S Finnclipper

Photo: © Maxofsweden/Wikimedia Commons/CC BY 3.0

Name of ship	M/S Finnclipper	

Home port / Flag state	Malmö / Sweden
Shipyard / Yard number	Astilleros Españoles, Puerto Real, Spain / #78
Previous ship names	-
Year of construction	1999

Call sign	SFZO	Classification	Registro Italiano Navale
IMO Number	9137997	**MMSI Number**	266192000
Length	188.30 m	**Gross tonnage**	33,958 BRZ
Beam	29.54 m	**Net tonnage**	10,214 NRZ
Draught	6.30 m	**Deadweight**	7,823 tdw
Passengers / Cabins	440 / 191	**Maximum speed**	22.1 kn
Vehicles	Unspecified	**Cargo capacity**	3,118 lm

Main engines	4 x Sulzer 8ZAL40S, Diesel / 23,040 kW
Auxiliary engines	3 x Diesel, 3,480 kW
Propeller	2 x Propeller, controllable pitch
Bow thruster	2 x Tunnel

Figure 78: M/S Finnfellow   Photo: © Johan Fredriksson/Wikimedia Commons/ CC BY 3.0

Name of ship	M/S Finnfellow

Home port / Flag state	Mariehamn / Finland
Shipyard / Yard number	Astilleros Españoles, Puerto Real, Spain / #80
Previous ship names	2000 - 2003 Stena Britannica
Year of construction	1999

Call sign	OJQC	Classification	Registro Italiano Navale
IMO Number	9145164	**MMSI Number**	230637000
Length	188.30 m	**Gross tonnage**	33,958 GT
Beam	29.54 m	**Net tonnage**	10,214 NT
Draught	6.30 m	**Deadweight**	7,823 tdw
Passengers / Cabins	395 / 186	**Maximum speed**	22.1 kn
Vehicles	Unspecified	**Cargo capacity**	3,118 lm

Main engines	4 x Sulzer 8ZAL40S, Diesel / 23,040 kW
Auxiliary engines	3 x Diesel, 3,480 kW
Propeller	2 x Propeller, controllable pitch
Bow thruster	2 x Tunnel

Figure 79: M/S Finnlady

Photo: © Finnlines

Name of ship — M/S Finnlady

Home port / Flag state	Mariehamn / Finland
Shipyard / Yard number	Fincantieri Cantieri Navali Italiani, Ancona, Italy / #6133
Previous ship names	2006-2007 Europalink (until delivery)
Year of construction	2007

Call sign	OJMQ	Classification	Det Norske Veritas
IMO Number	9336268	MMSI Number	230987000
Length	218.719 m	Gross tonnage	45,923 GT
Beam	30.52 m	Net tonnage	24,006 NT
Draught	7.10 m	Deadweight	9,653 tdw
Passengers / Cabins	500 / 201	Maximum speed	25 kn
Vehicles	Unspecified	Cargo capacity	4,200 lm

Main engines	4 x Wärtsilä 9R64, Diesel / 41,580 kW
Auxiliary engines	3 x Wärtsilä 6L20, Diesel
Propeller	2 x Prop., controllable pitch, Rolls-Royce 179XF5/4D-S/CSL/W
Bow thruster	2 x Rolls-Royce TT 2650 ICE CP, Tunnel

Figure 80: M/S Finnmaid   Photo: © Andrzej Otrębski/WikimediaCommons CC-BY-SA-3.0

Name of ship	M/S Finnmaid	

Home port / Flag state   Mariehamn / Finland

Shipyard / Yard number   Fincantieri Cantieri Navali, Castellamare, Italy / #6125

Previous ship names   -

Year of construction   2006

Call sign	OJMI	Classification	Det Norske Veritas
IMO Number	9319466	MMSI Number	230982000
Length	218.719 m	Gross tonnage	45,923 GT
Beam	30.52 m	Net tonnage	24,006 NT
Draught	7.10 m	Deadweight	9,653 tdw
Passengers / Cabins	500 / 201	Maximum speed	25 kn
Vehicles	Unspecified	Cargo capacity	4,200 lm

Main engines   4 x Wärtsilä 9R64, Diesel / 41,580 kW

Auxiliary engines   3 x Wärtsilä 6L20, Diesel

Propeller   2 x Prop., controllable pitch, Rolls-Royce 179XF5/4D-S/CSL/W

Bow thruster   2 x Rolls-Royce TT 2650 ICE CP, Tunnel

Figure 81: M/S Finnpartner   Photo: © Finnlines

Name of ship   M/S Finnpartner

Home port / Flag state	Malmö / Sweden
Shipyard / Yard number	Stocznia Gdanska S.A., Gdansk, Poland / # B501/02
Previous ship names	-
Year of construction	1994

Call sign	SKIH	Classification	Det Norske Veritas
IMO Number	9010163	MMSI Number	266262000
Length	183.00 m	Gross tonnage	32,534 GT
Beam	29.10 m	Net tonnage	9,761 NT
Draught	7.416 m	Deadweight	11,600 tdw
Passengers / Cabins	270 / 184	Maximum speed	21.3 kn
Vehicles	Unspecified	Cargo capacity	3,052 lm

Main engines	4 × Zgoda-Sulzer 8ZA40S, Diesel / 23,040 kW
Auxiliary engines	1 x Wärtsilä 4L20, 1 x Wärtsilä 8R 22HF, 1 x Wärtsilä 6R 22HF
Propeller	2 x Propeller, controllable pitch, Ulstein
Bow thruster	2 x Ulstein 90 TV-A, 2 x Stern thruster Ulstein 375 TV-C

Figure 82: M/S Finnstar

Photo: © Finnlines

Name of ship	M/S Finnstar	

Home port / Flag state	Mariehamn / Finland
Shipyard / Yard number	Fincantieri Cantieri Navali, Castellamare, Italy / #6123
Previous ship names	-
Year of construction	2006

Call sign	OJMH	Classification	Det Norske Veritas
IMO Number	9319442	**MMSI Number**	230981000
Length	218.719 m	**Gross tonnage**	45,923 GT
Beam	30.52 m	**Net tonnage**	24,006 NT
Draught	7.10 m	**Deadweight**	9,653 tdw
Passengers / Cabins	500 / 201	**Maximum speed**	25 kn
Vehicles	Unspecified	**Cargo capacity**	4,200 lm

Main engines	4 x Wärtsilä 9R64, Diesel / 41,580 kW
Auxiliary engines	3 x Wärtsilä 6L20, Diesel
Propeller	2 x Prop., controllable pitch, Rolls-Royce 179XF5/4D-S/CSL/W
Bow thruster	2 x Rolls-Royce TT 2650 ICE CP, Tunnel

Figure 83: M/S Finntrader

Photo: © Finnlines

Name of ship   M/S Finntrader

Home port / Flag state	Malmö / Sweden
Shipyard / Yard number	Stocznia Gdanska S.A., Gdansk, Poland / # B501/04
Previous ship names	-
Year of construction	1995

Call sign	SKIJ	**Classification**	Det Norske Veritas
IMO Number	9017769	**MMSI Number**	266239000
Length	183.00 m	**Gross tonnage**	32,534 GT
Beam	29.10 m	**Net tonnage**	9,761 NT
Draught	7.416 m	**Deadweight**	11,600 tdw
Passengers / Cabins	270 / 184	**Maximum speed**	21.3 kn
Vehicles	Unspecified	**Cargo capacity**	3,052 lm

Main engines	4 × Zgoda-Sulzer 8ZA40S, Diesel / 23,040 kW
Auxiliary engines	1 x Wärtsilä 4L20, 1 x Wärtsilä 8R 22HF, 1 x Wärtsilä 6R 22HF
Propeller	2 x Propeller, controllable pitch, Ulstein
Bow thruster	2 x Ulstein 90 TV-A, 2 x Stern thruster Ulstein 375 TV-C

Figure 84: M/S Nordlink   Photo: © Joeran/WikimediaCommons/CC-BY-SA-3.0

Name of ship	M/S Nordlink

Home port / Flag state	Malmö / Sweden
Shipyard / Yard number	Fincantieri Cantieri Navali, Ancona, Italy / #6134
Previous ship names	-
Year of construction	2007

Call sign	SJPW	Classification	Det Norske Veritas
IMO Number	9336256	**MMSI Number**	266252000
Length	218.79 m	**Gross tonnage**	45,923 GT
Beam	30.50 m	**Net tonnage**	24,006 NT
Draught	7.10 m	**Deadweight**	9,653 tdw
Passengers / Cabins	500 / 201	**Maximum speed**	25 kn
Vehicles	Unspecified	**Cargo capacity**	4,200 lm

Main engines	4 x Wärtsilä 9L46, Diesel / 41,580 kW
Auxiliary engines	3 x Wärtsilä 6L20, Diesel
Propeller	2 x Prop., controllable pitch, Rolls-Royce 179XF5/4D-S/CSL/W
Bow thruster	2 x Rolls-Royce TT 2650 ICE CP, Tunnel

fjordline com

Fjord Line was founded in 1993 as a subsidiary of Rutelaget Askøy Bergen AS, headquartered in Bergen, to start a new ferry connection to Denmark. Rutelaget Askøy Bergen was founded in 1950 for the local ferry service between the island Askøy and Bergen. In addition Rutelaget maintained a ferry service between Stavanger and Bergen as well as in the Boknafjord. In 1992 a new ferry service between Bergen and Egersund and Hanstholm in Denmark was introduced. In January 1, 1995 the Danish shipping company Fred.Olsen and the Norwegian Fjord Line merged under the auspices of Fjord Line. The joint company continued the business activities from then on under the name of Fjord Line AS. In the fall of 1998, Fjord Line took over from Color Line the ferry service between Bergen, Haugesund and Stavanger, which has already been served in the eighties of Fred. Olsen. In 2007 Fjord Line merged with the Norwegian shipping company Master Ferries, based in Kristiansand, Norway. The new company continued to wear the name of Fjord Line.

With the beginning of 2009, the traditional destinations Egersund and Hanstholm no longer were served, but Fjord Line revived with the M/S Bergensfjord the ferry connection between Hirtshals, Stavanger and Bergen. Since April 2010 the Fjord Line ferries again are going regularly between Denmark and Norway. With the commission of the new M/S Bergensfjord the former M/S Bergensfjord was taken out of service and put to extensive modification and modernization in the yard. Under the new name M/S Oslofjord she is scheduled for the traffic on the route Sandefjord (Norway) and Stromstad (Sweden) from June 2014. With this in 2014 for the first time a Swedish port is added to the route network of Fjord Line.

Figure 85: M/S Stavangerfjord

Photo: © Fjord Line/Espen Gees

Figure 86: M/S Bergensfjord   Photo: © Fjord Line/Espen Gees

Name of ship   M/S Bergensfjord   +

Home port / Flag state	Hirtshals / Denmark
Shipyard / Yard number	Stocznia Gdansk S.A., Gdansk, Poland / #88
Previous ship names	-
Year of construction	2014

Call sign	OYPJ2	Classification	Det Norske Veritas
IMO Number	9586617	MMSI Number	219348000
Length	170.00 m	Gross tonnage	31,678 GT
Beam	27.50 m	Net tonnage	14,270 NT
Draught	6.35 m	Deadweight	3,900 tdw
Passengers / Cabins	1,500 / 306	Maximum speed	21.5 kn
Vehicles	600 Cars	Cargo capacity	3,900 t

Main engines	4 x Bergen Engines B35:40V12PG, Diesel / each 5,600 kW
Auxiliary engines	2 x MAN 6L21/31, 1 x MAN 7L21/31 / 19,040 kW
Propeller	2 x Propeller, controllable pitch Rolls-Royce 111 A/4 D-ICE/B
Bow thruster	2 x Rolls-Royce TT 2400 AUX FP

Figure 87: HSC Fjord Cat   Photo: © Fjord Line A/S

Name of ship — HSC Fjord Cat

Home port / Flag state	Hirtshals / Denmark
Shipyard / Yard number	InCat Australia Pty Ltd, Hobart, Australia / #049
Previous ship names	1998-1999 Cat Link V,1999-2005, 2006 Mads Mols, 2005-2006 Incat 049, 2006-2008 Master Cat
Year of construction	1998

Call sign	OZCR2	**Classification**	Det Norske Veritas
IMO Number	9176060	**MMSI Number**	220574000
Length	91.30 m	**Gross tonnage**	5,619 GT
Beam	26.00 m	**Net tonnage**	2,314 NT
Draught	3.70 m	**Deadweight**	500 tdw
Passengers	686	**Maximum speed**	48.2 kn
Vehicles	240 Cars	**Cargo capacity**	No Freight

Main engines	4 × Ruston 20RK 270M MKII, Diesel, each 7,082 kW
Auxiliary engines	4 x Caterpillar, Diesel, each 1,028 kW
Propeller	4 x Waterjet

Figure 88: M/S Oslofjord   Photo: © Fjord Line A/S

Name of ship   M/S Oslofjord   ✚

Home port / Flag state	Hirtshals / Denmark
Shipyard / Yard number	Fosen Mekaniske Verksteder AS, Rissa, Norway / #52
Previous ship names	1993-2003 Bergen, 2003-2005 Duchess of Scandinavia, 2005-2008 Atlantic Traveller, 2008-2014 Bergensfjord
Year of construction	1993

Call sign	OUZI 2	Classification	Det Norske Veritas
IMO Number	9058995	**MMSI Number**	219002929
Length	134.40 m	**Gross tonnage**	16,794 GT
Beam	24.0 m	**Net tonnage**	6,082 NT
Draught	5.70 m	**Deadweight**	3,200 tdw
Passengers	1,800	**Maximum speed**	19.0 kn
Vehicles	370 Cars	**Cargo capacity**	720 lm

Main engines	2 x Wärtsilä-Sulzer 8ZA40S, Diesel / 11,520 kW
Auxiliary engines	3 x Mitsubishi S6R2, Diesel
Propeller	2 x Wichmann Propeller, controllable pitch
Bow thruster	2 x Brunvoll FU 80 LTC 2250, Tunnel

Figure 89: M/S Stavangerfjord

Name of ship	M/S Stavangerfjord	

Home port / Flag state	Hirtshals / Denmark
Shipyard / Yard number	Stocznia Gdansk S.A., Gdansk, Poland / #87
Previous ship names	-
Year of construction	2013

Call sign	OYOW2	**Classification**	Det Norske Veritas
IMO Number	9586605	**MMSI Number**	219347000
Length	170.00 m	**Gross tonnage**	31,678 GT
Beam	27.50 m	**Net tonnage**	14,270 NT
Draught	6.35 m	**Deadweight**	3,900 tdw
Passengers / Cabins	1,500 / 306	**Maximum speed**	21.5 kn
Vehicles	600 Cars	**Cargo capacity**	3,900 t

Main engines	4 x Bergen Engines B35:40V12PG, Diesel / each 5,600 kW
Auxiliary engines	2 x MAN 6L21/31, 1 x MAN 7L21/31 / 19,040 kW
Propeller	2 x Propeller, controllable pitch Rolls-Royce 111 A/4 D-ICE/B
Bow thruster	2 x Rolls-Royce TT 2400 AUX FP

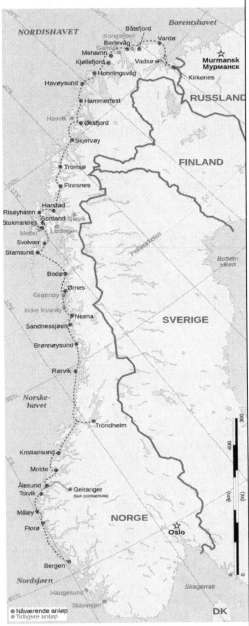

End of the 19th century the Norwegian government had the intention to connect the southern and the northern part of the country. Captain Richard With and Andreas Holthe took the challenge to map the Norwegian coast. Captain Richard With established in 1893 a regular service several times a week with his steam-boat "Vesteraalen", first between Trondheim and Hammerfest and later between Bergen and Kirkenes. Because of the at this time very short travel time of 7 days he himself called the route "fast route" in Norwegian "Hurtigruten". During the Second World War several Hurtigruten ships were used by the Norwegian government for transport tasks. 9 of the 15 used Hurtigruten ships were lost during the war. So, in 1945 the reconstruction of the Hurtigruten line had highest priority. During the following years, only ships with modern diesel propulsion were put into service. With this the era of steam shipping was finished. Hurtigruten now covered again the traffic from Bergen to Kirkenes with 11 ships. Between 1993 and 2003 nine of the 11 ships were replaced by more modern units. 2006 OVDS and TFDS Hurtigruten merged to Hurtigruten ASA. In 2007, Hurtigruten commissioned the M/S Fram, an expedition ship without car capacity for tours to Greenland, Antarctica and to Spitsbergen. [23]

Figure 91: M/S Finnmarken

Photo: © Aldebaran / Wikimedia Commons CC-BY-SA-3.0

Name of ship — M/S Finnmarken

Home port / Flag state	Tromsø / Norway
Shipyard / Yard number	Kleven Verft A/S, Ulsteinvik, Norway / #292
Previous ship names	-
Year of construction	2002

Call sign	LDBE	Classification	Det Norske Veritas
IMO Number	9231951	**MMSI Number**	259210000
Length	138.50 m	**Gross tonnage**	15,690 GT
Beam	21.50 m	**Net tonnage**	6,113 NT
Draught	4.80 m	**Deadweight**	945 tdw
Passengers / Cabins	1,000 / 283	**Maximum speed**	19 kn
Vehicles	47 Cars	**Cargo capacity**	Unspecified

Main engines	2 x Wärtsilä 9L32, Diesel / each 4,140 kW
Auxiliary engines	2 x Wärtsilä 6L32, Diesel / each 2,760 kW
Propeller	2 x Propeller, controllable pitch, Wärtsilä Propulsion
Bow thruster	2 x Brunvoll FU80LTC 2250, Tunnel / each 1,000 kW 1 x Stern thruster 360°Azimuth (Propac) / 1,200 kW

Figure 92: M/S Kong Harald

Name of ship	M/S Kong Harald	

Home port / Flag state	Tromsø / Norway
Shipyard / Yard number	Volkswerft GmbH, Stralsund, Germany / #101
Previous ship names	-
Year of construction	1993

Call sign	LGIY	Classification	Det Norske Veritas
IMO Number	9039119	**MMSI Number**	257200000
Length	121.80 m	**Gross tonnage**	11,204 GT
Beam	23.40 m	**Net tonnage**	4,153 NT
Draught	4.70 m	**Deadweight**	902 tdw
Passengers / Berths	622 / 474	**Maximum speed**	18 kn
Vehicles	45 Cars	**Cargo capacity**	1,500 m³

Main engines	2 x MAK 6M552C, Diesel / each 4,500 kW
Auxiliary engines	2 x BMV KRG-8, Diesel
Propeller	2 x Propeller, controllable pitch KaMeWa 94XF3/4
Bow thruster	2 x Brunvoll FU63LTC, Tunnel / 1 x Stern thruster Ulstein TCNS 73/50 (COMPASS)

Figure 93: M/S Lofoten

Photo: © Aldebaran / Wikimedia Commons CC-BY-SA-3.0

Name of ship	M/S Lofoten

Home port / Flag state	Tromsø / Norway
Shipyard / Yard number	Akers Mekaniske Verksted, Oslo, Norway / #547
Previous ship names	-
Year of construction	1964

Call sign	LIXN	**Classification**	Det Norske Veritas
IMO Number	5424562	**MMSI Number**	258477000
Length	87.41 m	**Gross tonnage**	2,621 GT
Beam	13.28 m	**Net tonnage**	1,099 NT
Draught	4.622 m	**Deadweight**	671 tdw
Passengers / Berths	410 / 184	**Maximum speed**	16 kn
Vehicles	Unspecified	**Cargo capacity**	Unspecified

Main engines	1 x B &W DM 742 VT2BF.90, Diesel / 2,480 kW
Auxiliary engines	1 x Volvo Penta D30A-MT / 2 x BMV RTGB-3, Diesel
Propeller	2 x Propeller, controllable pitch A.M. Liaaen
Bow thruster	Unspecified

Figure 94: M/S Midnatsol   Photo: © Hurtigruten / Dr. Christa Imkamp

Name of ship   M/S Midnatsol

Home port / Flag state	Tromsø / Norway
Shipyard / Yard number	Fosen Mekaniske Verksteder AS, Rissa, Norway / #73
Previous ship names	-
Year of construction	2003

Call sign	LMDH	Classification	Det Norske Veritas
IMO Number	9247728	MMSI Number	258595000
Length	135.75 m	Gross tonnage	16,151 GT
Beam	21.50 m	Net tonnage	6,353 NT
Draught	5.10 m	Deadweight	1,184 tdw
Passengers / Cabins	1,000 / 302	Maximum speed	18.5 kn
Vehicles	45 Cars	Cargo capacity	N/A

Main engines	2 x Wärtsilä 9L32, Diesel / 8,280 kW
Auxiliary engines	2 x Caterpillar 3516 B DITA, Diesel
Propeller	2 x Pods (Propeller nacelles) Rolls-Royce Contaz 35
Bow thruster	2 x Brunvoll FU80 LTC 2250 / each 1,200 kW 1 x Brunvoll FU63 LTC 1750 / 900 kW

Figure 95: M/S Nordkapp

Photo: © M.Prinke / Wikimedia Commons CC-BY-SA 2.0

Name of ship	M/S Nordkapp	

Home port / Flag state	Tromsø / Norway
Shipyard / Yard number	Kværner Kleven Ulstein A/S, Ulstein, Norway / #265
Previous ship names	-
Year of construction	1996

Call sign	LASQ	Classification	Det Norske Veritas
IMO Number	9107772	**MMSI Number**	259330000
Length	123.30 m	**Gross tonnage**	11,386 GT
Beam	19.50 m	**Net tonnage**	4,210 NT
Draught	4.70 m	**Deadweight**	1,104 tdw
Passengers / Cabins	691 / 218	**Maximum speed**	19 kn
Vehicles	45 Cars	**Cargo capacity**	Unspecified

Main engines	2 x Krupp MAK 6M552C, Diesel / each 4,500 kW
Auxiliary engines	2 x Ulstein KRG-8, Diesel / each 1,265 kW
Propeller	2 x Propeller, controllable pitch KaMeWa 94XF3/4
Bow thruster	2 x Brunvoll FU45LTC1375, Tunnel / each 790 kW

Figure 96: M/S Nordlys

Photo: © Aldebaran / Wikimedia Commons CC BY-SA 3.0

Name of ship — M/S Nordlys

Home port / Flag state	Tromsø / Norway
Shipyard / Yard number	Volkswerft GmbH, Stralsund, Germany / #102
Previous ship names	-
Year of construction	1994

Call sign	LHCW	**Classification**	Det Norske Veritas
IMO Number	9048914	**MMSI Number**	259139000
Length	121.80 m	**Gross tonnage**	11,204 GT
Beam	23.783 m	**Net tonnage**	4,153 NT
Draught	4.70 m	**Deadweight**	850 tdw
Passengers / Berths	622 / 469	**Maximum speed**	18 kn
Vehicles	45 Cars	**Cargo capacity**	3 Stowages with 791 m³

Main engines	2 x MAK 6M552C, Diesel / each 4.500 kW
Auxiliary engines	2 x BMV KRG-8, Diesel
Propeller	2 x Propeller, controllable pitch KaMeWa 94XF3/4
Bow thruster	2 x Brunvoll FU63 LTC, Tunnel / 790 kW

Figure 97: M/S Nordnorge

Name of ship	M/S Nordnorge

Home port / Flag state	Tromsø / Norway
Shipyard / Yard number	Kværner Kleven Ulstein A/S, Ulstein, Norway / #266
Previous ship names	-
Year of construction	1997

Call sign	3YGW	Classification	Det Norske Veritas
IMO Number	9107784	MMSI Number	259371000
Length	123.30 m	Gross tonnage	11,384 GT
Beam	19.50 m	Net tonnage	4,209 NT
Draught	4.70 m	Deadweight	1,171 tdw
Passengers / Cabins	691 / 214	Maximum speed	18.7 kn
Vehicles	45 Cars	Cargo capacity	Unspecified

Main engines	2 x Krupp MAK 6M552C, Diesel / each 4,500 kW
Auxiliary engines	2 x Ulstein KRG-8, Diesel / each 1,265 kW
Propeller	2 x Propeller, controllable pitch KaMeWa 94XF3/4
Bow thruster	2 x Brunvoll FU45LTC1375, Tunnel / each 790 kW 2 x Stern thruster Brunvoll FU63LTC1750/ each 790 kW

Figure 98: M/S Polarlys

Name of ship	M/S Polarlys

Home port / Flag state	Tromsø / Norway
Shipyard / Yard number	Ulstein Verft A/S, Ulsteinvik, Norway / #223
Previous ship names	-
Year of construction	1996

Call sign	LHYG	**Classification**	Det Norske Veritas
IMO Number	9107796	**MMSI Number**	259322000
Length	123.00 m	**Gross tonnage**	11,341 GT
Beam	19.50 m	**Net tonnage**	4,171 NT
Draught	4.70 m	**Deadweight**	1,150 tdw
Passengers / Cabins	737 / 225	**Maximum speed**	19 kn
Vehicles	35 Cars	**Cargo capacity**	Unspecified

Main engines	2 x Ulstein KRG-9 and 2 x Ulstein BRM-9
Auxiliary engines	Unspecified
Propeller	2 x Propeller, controllable pitch
Bow thruster	2 x Rolls-Royce 375 TV, Tunnel + 1 Stern thruster

Figure 99: M/S Richard With

Photo: © Hurtigruten / Meegan Parkee

| Name of ship | M/S Richard With | |

Home port / Flag state	Narvik / Norway
Shipyard / Yard number	Volkswerft GmbH, Stralsund, Germany / #103
Previous ship names	-
Year of construction	1993

Call sign	LGWH	Classification	Det Norske Veritas
IMO Number	9040429	MMSI Number	258500000
Length	121.80 m	Gross tonnage	11,205 GT
Beam	23.40 m	Net tonnage	4,153 NT
Draught	4.70 m	Deadweight	850 tdw
Passengers / Berths	623 / 464	Maximum speed	15 kn
Vehicles	45 Cars	Cargo capacity	3 Cooling rooms with 785 m³ + Cargo 1,700 m³

Main engines	2 x MAK 6M552C, Diesel / each 4,500 kW
Auxiliary engines	2 x BMV KRG-8, Diesel
Propeller	2 x Propeller, controllable pitch KaMeWa 94XF3/4
Bow thruster	2 x Brunvoll FU63 LTC, Tunnel / 790 kW

Figure 100: M/S Trollfjord

Photo: © Hurtigruten / Nina Helland

Name of ship	M/S Trollfjord

Home port / Flag state   Tromsø / Norway

Shipyard / Yard number   Fosen Mekaniske Verksteder AS, Rissa, Norway / #72

Previous ship names   -

Year of construction   2002

Call sign	LLVT	Classification	Det Norske Veritas
IMO Number	9233258	MMSI Number	258465000
Length	135.75 m	Gross tonnage	16,140 GT
Beam	21.50 m	Net tonnage	6,291 NT
Draught	5.10 m	Deadweight	1,180 tdw
Passengers / Cabins	822 / 301	Maximum speed	18.5 kn
Vehicles	45 Cars	Cargo capacity	N/A

Main engines   2 x Wärtsilä 9L32, Diesel / 8,280 kW

Auxiliary engines   2 x Caterpillar 3516 B DITA, Diesel

Propeller   2 x Pods (Propeller nacelles) Rolls-Royce Contaz 35

Bow thruster   2 x Brunvoll FU80 LTC 2250 / each 1,200 kW
1 x Brunvoll FU63 LTC 1750 / 900 kW

Figure 101: M/S Vesterålen   Photo: © Aldebaran / Wikimedia Commons CC-BY-SA-3.0

Name of ship   M/S Vesterålen

Home port / Flag state   Tromsø / Norway

Shipyard / Yard number   Kaarbøs Mekaniske Verksted ,Harstad, Norway / #101

Previous ship names   -

Year of construction   1983

Call sign	LLZY	Classification	Det Norske Veritas
IMO Number	8019368	MMSI Number	258478000
Length	108.55 m	Gross tonnage	6,261 GT
Beam	16.52 m	Net tonnage	2,257 NT
Draught	4.60 m	Deadweight	900 tdw
Passengers / Berths	510 / 294	Maximum speed	19 kn
Vehicles	35 Cars	Cargo capacity	Unspecified

Main engines   2 x BMV KVM-16, Diesel / each 2,380 kW

Auxiliary engines   2 x BMV KRG-5, Diesel / 1 x BMV KRG-3, Diesel

Propeller   2 x Propeller, controllable pitch Ulstein 85/4-300

Bow thruster   2 x Brunvoll SPT-VP-400

Figure 102: Irish Ferries Fleet   Photo: © Irish Ferries

IRISH FERRIES

Irish Ferries is part of the Irish Continental Group and operates four ferries on international routes between Ireland, Britain and France, transporting passengers, vehicles and freight units. The history of Irish Ferries is going back to 1973 when Irish Continental Line was formed as a joint venture between the Irish Shipping Limited, Fearnley & Eger and the Swedish Lion Ferry. When Irish Shipping Limited went into liquidation in 1984, Irish Continental Line was transforming in a management buyout to Irish Continental Group. In 1992, the Irish Continental Group took over the B+I Line (British and Irish Steam Packet Company) with routes between Dublin and Holyhead as well as Rosslare and Pembroke Dock. In the following years the Irish Continental Group invested more than 500 million Euros to replace the aging fleet with today one of the most modern ferry fleets in Europe. New ferries were built and taken into service on the Irish Sea and between Ireland and the French ports of Roscoff and Cherbourg. There are the M/S Oscar Wilde on it's route from Rosslare (Ireland) to Cherbourg (France) and the M/S Epsilon from Rosslare (Ireland) to Roscoff (France), further the M/S Ulysses on the Irish Sea be used on the Rosslare – Roscoff route the Ulysses, the Dublin Swift on the Dublin – Holyhead route and the Isle of Inishmore on the Pembroke - Rosslare route. [24]

Figure 103: M/S Epsilon
Photo: © Irish Ferries

Name of ship — M/S Epsilon

Home port / Flag state	Bari / Italy
Shipyard / Yard number	Cantiere Navale Visentini, Porto Viro, Italy / #228
Previous ship names	2011-2013 Cartour Epsilon
Year of construction	2011

Call sign	ICRB	**Classification**	Registro Italiano Navale
IMO Number	9539054	**MMSI Number**	247297100
Length	186.50 m	**Gross tonnage**	26,375 GT
Beam	25.60 m	**Net tonnage**	Unspecified
Draught	6.85 m	**Deadweight**	8,615 tdw
Passengers / Cabins	500 / 70	**Maximum speed**	24 kn
Vehicles	74 Cars	**Cargo capacity**	2,859 lm

Main engines	2 x MAN B&W, Diesel / 10,800 kW
Auxiliary engines	2 x Diesel / each 1,800 kW
Propeller	2 x Propeller, controllable pitch
Bow thruster	2 x Tunnel / each 1.300 kW

Figure 104: M/S Oscar Wilde

Photo: © Irish Ferries

Name of ship — M/S Oscar Wilde

Home port / Flag state   Nassau / Bahamas

Shipyard / Yard number   Wärtsilä Marine Yard, Åbo, Finland / #1292

Previous ship names   1987-2007 Kronprins Harald

Year of construction   1987

Call sign	C6WL9	Classification	Lloyd's Register of Shipping
IMO Number	8506311	MMSI Number	308847000
Length	166,30 m	Gross tonnage	31,914 GT
Beam	28.41 m	Net tonnage	17,126 NT
Draught	6.50 m	Deadweight	4,606 tdw
Passengers / Berths	1,440 / 1,440	Maximum speed	22 kn
Vehicles	700 Cars	Cargo capacity	1,220 lm

Main engines   2 x Sulzer-Wärtsilä 12 ZAV 40, Diesel / 19,800 kW

Auxiliary engines   2 x Sulzer-Wärtsilä 6 ZAL 40, Diesel

Propeller   2 x Propeller, controllable pitch

Bow thruster   2 x Tunnel

Figure 105: M/S Princess Anastasia in the port of Tallinn 2017   Photo: © Pjotr Mahhonin / Wiki Commons CC-BY.SA 4.0

Moby SPL Limited was founded in 2016 in St.Petersburg (Russia) as merger between the Italian Moby Lines and the Russian St.Peter Line.

Moby Lines is currently the biggest Italian ferry operator with a long history, serving in the Mediterranean just since 1956. St.Peter Line was founded in 2010 in Cyprus from Russian, Swiss and EU-based investors. The headquarter of the shipping company is located in St.Petersburg (Russia).

Moby SPL operates as passenger and freight line with the ro-pax ferry M/S Princess Anastasia and connects St.Petersburg via Helsinki (Finland) with Stockholm (Sweden) and via Helsinki (Finland) with Tallinn (Estonia). [25]

Figure 106: M/S Princess Anastasia   Photo: © Pjotr Mahhonin / Wikimedia Commons CC-BY-SA 4.0

Name of ship	M/S Princess Anastasia	

Home port / Flag state	Napoli / Italy
Shipyard / Yard number	Oy Wärtsilä Ab, Åbo, Finland / #1290
Previous ship names	1986-1993 Olympia, 1993-2010 Pride of Bilbao, 2010-2013 Bilbao, 2013-2017 SPL Princess Anastasia
Year of construction	1986

Call sign	9HA2705	Classification	Lloyd´s Register of Shipping
IMO Number	8414582	MMSI Number	215357000
Length	177.10 m	Gross tonnage	37,583 GT
Beam	28.46 m	Net tonnage	23,730 NT
Draught	6.70 m	Deadweight	3,898 tdw
Passengers / Cabins	2,500 / 834	Maximum speed	22 kn
Vehicles	580 Cars	Cargo capacity	1,115 lm

Main engines	4xWärtsila-Pielstick 12PC2-6V,Diesel / each 5,750kW
Auxiliary engines	Unspecified
Propeller	2 x Propeller, controllable pitch
Bow thruster	2 x Tunnel

P & O can already look back on a long history that began in the late 60s with the establishment of ferry services in the North Sea and the English Channel. In the late 70s also P&O was not spared out from the crisis in the traditional shipping business and decided to separe from some business areas, including the ferry services between Dover (United Kingdom) and Boulogne (France) and from Southampton (United Kingdom) to Le Havre (France) in 1985, which were sold to European Ferries. In January 1986, P&O took over 50.01 % of the European Financial Holdings Ltd., which was holding 20.8 % of European Ferries. The following year, P&O took over the remaining shares in European Ferries Group whose ferry activities were named Townsend Thoresen. After the name Townsend Thoresen was negatively affected by the disaster of the "Herald of Free Enterprise" in March 1987, in which 187 people died, the company was renamed on October 22, 1987 in P&O European Ferries.

On November 28, 1996 P & O European Ferries was split into three separate companies: P&O Porthsmouth, the P&O North Sea and in collaboration with Stena Line the joint venture P&O Stena Line , based in Dover. In August 2002, P&O took over the 40% joint venture share of Stena Line. With the merger of P&O North Sea, P&O Porthsmouth and now the wholly P&O owned P&O Stena Line in October 2002 a new ferry company was born : the P&O Ferries Ltd., based in Dover. As a result of declining passenger numbers by the spread of low-cost airlines as well as the increasing use of the Eurotunnel under the English Channel various routes out of Porthsmouth were reviewed in the fall of 2004. At the end remained only the route Portsmouth-Bilbao, which was still in operation until the end of September 2010. With the expiry of the charter contract for the "Pride of Bilbao", at the same time the last remaining route from Porthsmouth was cancelled. Today, P&O Ferries operates regularly between the United Kingdom and Ireland, as well as between the United Kingdom and France, Belgium and the Netherlands. [26]

Figure 107: M/S Pride of Bruges   Photo: © P&O Ferries

Name of ship — M/S Pride of Bruges

Home port / Flag state	Rotterdam / Netherlands
Shipyard / Yard number	Nippon Kokan, Tsurumi Shipyard, Yokohama, Japan/ #1033
Previous ship names	1987-2003 Norsun
Year of construction	1987

Call sign	PGJW	Classification	Lloyd´s Register of Shipping
IMO Number	8503797	**MMSI Number**	244387000
Length	179.35 m	**Gross tonnage**	31,598 GT
Beam	25.09 m	**Net tonnage**	18,174 NT
Draught	6.187 m	**Deadweight**	6,748 tdw
Passengers / Berths	1050 / 930	**Maximum speed**	18.5 kn
Vehicles	850 Cars	**Cargo capacity**	2,250 lm

Main engines	4 x Sulzer SWD 16TM410, Diesel / 19,200 kW
Auxiliary engines	Unspecified
Propeller	2 x Propeller, controllable pitch
Bow thruster	2 x Tunnel

Figure 108: M/S Pride of Burgundy   Photo: © Paul Dashwood / PD

Name of ship   M/S Pride of Burgundy

Home port / Flag state   Dover / United Kingdom

Shipyard / Yard number   Schichau Seebeckwerft, Bremerhaven, Germany/ #1078

Previous ship names   1993-1998 European Causeway,
1998-2002 P&OSL Burgundy, 2002-2003 PO Burgundy

Year of construction   1993

Call sign	MQSQ9	Classification	Lloyd's Register of Shipping
IMO Number	9015254	MMSI Number	232001470
Length	179.40 m	Gross tonnage	28,138 GT
Beam	28.30 m	Net tonnage	Unspecified
Draught	6.25 m	Deadweight	5,812 tdw
Passengers	1,420	Maximum speed	21 kn
Vehicles	600 Cars	Cargo capacity	1,925 lm or 120 Lorries

Main engines   4 x Sulzer 8ZA40S, Diesel / each 5,280 kW

Auxiliary engines   4 x Sulzer 6ATL25H, Diesel / each 1,150 kW

Propeller   1 x Caterpillar 3412 D1-AT

Bow thruster   2 x Lips 1,200 kW, Tunnel

Figure 109: M/S Pride of Canterbury

Photo: © P&O Ferries

Name of ship	M/S Pride of Canterbury	

Home port / Flag state Dover / United Kingdom

Shipyard / Yard number Schichau Seebeckwerft, Bremerhaven, Germany/ #1076

Previous ship names 1991-2003 European Pathway

Year of construction 1991

Call sign	MPQZ6	Classification	Lloyd's Register of Shipping
IMO Number	9007295	MMSI Number	232001060
Length	179.70 m	Gross tonnage	28,138 GT
Beam	23.30 m	Net tonnage	8,649 NT
Draught	6.27 m	Deadweight	5,875 tdw
Passengers	2,000	Maximum speed	21 kn
Vehicles	550 Cars	Cargo capacity	1,725 lm or 115 Lorries

Main engines 4 x Sulzer 8ZA40S, Diesel / each 5,280kW

Auxiliary engines 4 x Sulzer 6ATL25H, Diesel / each 1,150 kW

Propeller 1 x Caterpillar 3412 D1-AT

Bow thruster 2 x Lips 1,200 kW, Tunnel

Figure 110: M/S Pride of Hull

Photo: © P&O Ferries

Name of ship — M/S Pride of Hull ▶

Home port / Flag state	Nassau / Bahamas
Shipyard / Yard number	Fincantieri SpA., Porto Maghera, Venice, Italy / #6066
Previous ship names	-
Year of construction	2001

Call sign	C6ZQ4	**Classification**	Lloyd's Register of Shipping
IMO Number	9208629	**MMSI Number**	235249000
Length	215.44 m	**Gross tonnage**	59,925 GT
Beam	31.502 m	**Net tonnage**	Unspecified
Draught	6.30 m	**Deadweight**	8,850 tdw
Passengers / Cabins	1,360 / 546	**Maximum speed**	22 kn
Vehicles	125 Cars	**Cargo capacity**	3,300 lm or 285 Trailers

Main engines	4 × Wärtsilä 9L46C, Diesel / each 9,350 kW
Auxiliary engines	2 x Wärtsilä 9L32, Diesel / 4,050 kW
Propeller	2 x Propeller, controllable pitch
Bow thruster	2 x Tunnel / 2,000 kW

Figure 111: M/S Pride of Kent
Photo: © Alf van Beem / Wikimedia Commons CC-Zero

Name of ship	M/S Pride of Kent	

Home port / Flag state	Dover / United Kingdom
Shipyard / Yard number	Schichau Seebeckwerft, Bremerhaven, Germany/ #1073
Previous ship names	1992-2003 European Highway
Year of construction	1992

Call sign	MQCJ2	**Classification**	Lloyd's Register of Shipping
IMO Number	9015266	**MMSI Number**	233009000
Length	179.70 m	**Gross tonnage**	28,138 GT
Beam	23.30 m	**Net tonnage**	8,649 NT
Draught	6.27 m	**Deadweight**	5,875 tdw
Passengers	2,000	**Maximum speed**	21 kn
Vehicles	550 Cars	**Cargo capacity**	1,725 lm or 115 Lorries

Main engines	4 x Sulzer, Diesel / each 5,280kW
Auxiliary engines	4 x Sulzer 6ATL25H, Diesel / each 1,150 kW
Propeller	1 x Caterpillar 3412 D1-AT
Bow thruster	2 x Lips 1,200 kW, Tunnel

Figure 112: M/S Pride of Rotterdam   Photo: © P&O Ferries

Name of ship   M/S Pride of Rotterdam

Home port / Flag state	Rotterdam / Netherlands
Shipyard / Yard number	Fincantieri SpA., Porto Maghera, Venice, Italy / #6065
Previous ship names	-
Year of construction	2001

Call sign	PBAJ	**Classification**	Lloyd's Register of Shipping
IMO Number	9208617	**MMSI Number**	244980000
Length	215.44 m	**Gross tonnage**	59,925 GT
Beam	31.502 m	**Net tonnage**	Unspecified
Draught	6.30 m	**Deadweight**	8,850 tdw
Passengers / Cabins	1,360 / 546	**Maximum speed**	22 kn
Vehicles	125 Cars	**Cargo capacity**	3,300 lm or 285 Trailers

Main engines	4 × Wärtsilä 9L46C, Diesel / each 9,350 kW
Auxiliary engines	2 x Wärtsilä 9L32, Diesel / 4,050 kW
Propeller	2 x Propeller, controllable pitch
Bow thruster	2 x Tunnel / 2,000 kW

Figure 113: M/S Pride of York   Photo: © Andy Beecroft / Wikimedia Commons CC-BY-SA-2.0

Name of ship	M/S Pride of York	

Home port / Flag state	Nassau / Bahamas
Shipyard / Yard number	Govan Shipbuilders Ltd, Glasgow, Scotland / #265
Previous ship names	1987-2003 Norsea
Year of construction	1987

Call sign	C6ZQ7	Classification	Lloyd's Register of Shipping
IMO Number	8501957	MMSI Number	311063300
Length	179.20 m	Gross tonnage	31,785 GT
Beam	25.40 m	Net tonnage	18,197 NT
Draught	6.13 m	Deadweight	6,545 tdw
Passengers	1,258	Maximum speed	19 kn
Vehicles	850 Cars	Cargo capacity	2,250 lm

Main engines	2 x Wärtsilä Sulzer 9ZAL40, Diesel / 18,390 kW
Auxiliary engines	2 x Wärtsilä Sulzer 6ZAL40, Diesel
Propeller	2 x Propeller, controllable pitch
Bow thruster	2 x Tunnel

Figure 114: M/S Spirit of Britain

Photo: © P&O Ferries

Name of ship	M/S Spirit of Britain	

Home port / Flag state	Dover / United Kingdom
Shipyard / Yard number	STX Europe New Shipyard, Helsinki, Finland / #1367
Previous ship names	-
Year of construction	2011

Call sign	2DXD4	Classification	Lloyd's Register of Shipping
IMO Number	9524231	MMSI Number	235082716
Length	213.00 m	Gross tonnage	47,592 GT
Beam	31.40 m	Net tonnage	14,277 NT
Draught	6.50 m	Deadweight	9,188 tdw
Passengers	2,000	Maximum speed	22 kn
Vehicles	1,059 Cars	Cargo capacity	2,700 lm or 180 Lorries

Main engines	4 x MAN 7L48/60, Diesel / each 7,600 kW
Auxiliary engines	4 x MAN, Diesel / each 1,424 kW
Propeller	2 x 4-Blade Propeller, controllable pitch MAN
Bow thruster	3 x Wärtsilä / 3,000 kW

Figure 115: M/S Spirit of France   Photo: © Davy-62 / Wikimedia Commons CC-BY-SA-3.0

Name of ship	M/S Spirit of France	

Home port / Flag state	Dover / United Kingdom
Shipyard / Yard number	STX Europe, Rauma, Finland / #1368
Previous ship names	-
Year of construction	2012

Call sign	2DXD5	Classification	Lloyd's Register of Shipping
IMO Number	9533816	MMSI Number	235082717
Length	213.00 m	Gross tonnage	47,592 GT
Beam	31.40 m	Net tonnage	14,277 NT
Draught	6.50 m	Deadweight	9,188 tdw
Passengers	2,000	Maximum speed	22 kn
Vehicles	1,059 Cars	Cargo capacity	2,700 lm or 180 Lorries

Main engines	4 x MAN 7L48/60, Diesel / each 7,600 kW
Auxiliary engines	4 x MAN, Diesel / each 1,424 kW
Propeller	2 x 4-Blade Propeller, controllable pitch MAN
Bow thruster	3 x Wärtsilä / 3,000 kW

Figure 116: Polferries fleet in the port of Świnoujście

Photo: © Mateusz War. / Wikimedia Commons / CC-BY-SA-3.0

Polferries (Polish Baltic Shipping Company) was founded as a Polish state-owned company under the name Polish Baltic Shipping (Polish Baltic shipping company) to establish a ferry service between Poland and Scandinavia on 31 January 1976. In 1992 Polferries received full legal recognition as a commercial ferry company based on the Western model. Polferries operates with three Ro-Pax-ferries on the Baltic Sea routes between the Swedish port of Nynäshamn, located near Stockholm and the Polish port of Gdansk and between Ystad in Southern Sweden and the Polish Baltic Sea port of Świnoujście. [27]

Figure 117: M/S Scandinavia arriving at the port of Gdansk

Photo: © Szilas / Wikimedia Commons CC-0

Figure 118: M/S Baltivia   Photo: © Brosen / Wikimedia Commons CC-BY-SA 3.0

Name of ship   M/S Baltivia

Home port / Flag state	Nassau / Bahamas
Shipyard / Yard number	Fartygsentreprenader AB, Uddevalla, Sweden / #153 Kalmar Varv A/B, Kalmar, Sweden / #453
Previous ship names	1981-1989 Sagaland, 1989-1993 Girolata, 1993-2002 Saga Star, 2002-2006 Dieppe
Year of construction	1981

Call sign	C6WN5	Classification	Det Norske Veritas
IMO Number	7931997	**MMSI Number**	309826000
Length	146,90 m	**Gross tonnage**	17,790 GT
Beam	24.00 m	**Net tonnage**	9,056 NT
Draught	6.25 m	**Deadweight**	5,309 tdw
Passengers / Berths	250 / 178	**Maximum speed**	20 kn
Vehicles	30 Cars	**Cargo capacity**	1,408 lm or 80 Lorries

Main engines	4 x Lindholmen-Pielstick 8PC2-5L, Diesel / each 3,310 kW
Auxiliary engines	3 x Diesel / each 1,058 kW
Propeller	2 x Propeller, controllable pitch
Bow thruster	2 x Tunnel / each 735 kW

Figure 119: M/S Mazovia

Photo: © Barabola / Wikimedia Commons CC BY-SA 4.0

Name of ship	M/S Mazovia	

Home port / Flag state	Nassau / Bahamas
Shipyard / Yard number	Pt Dok Kodja Bahri, Jakarta, Indonesia / #1005
Previous ship names	1996-1997 Gotland, 1997-2013 Finnarrow, 2013-2014 Euroferry Brindisi
Year of construction	1996

Call sign	C6BP8	**Classification**	Registro Navale Italiano
IMO Number	9010814	**MMSI Number**	311000330
Length	168.15 m	**Gross tonnage**	29,940 GT
Beam	28.30 m	**Net tonnage**	7,798 NT
Draught	6.60 m	**Deadweight**	6,124 tdw
Passengers	1,000	**Maximum speed**	21 kn
Vehicles	800 Cars	**Cargo capacity**	2,400 lm

Main engines	4 x Sulzer 6ZA40S, Diesel / 17,280 kW
Propeller	2 x Propeller, controllable pitch
Bow thruster	2 x Tunnel

Figure 120: M/S Wawel   Photo: © Brosen / Wikimedia Commons CC-BY-SA 3.0

Name of ship   M/S Wawel

Home port / Flag state	Nassau / Bahamas
Shipyard / Yard number	Kockums Varv AB, Malmö, Sweden / #569
Previous ship names	1980-1982 Scandinavia, 1982-1988 Tzarevetz, 1988-1990 Fiesta, 1990-1990 Fantasia, 1990-1998 Stena Fantasia, 1998-2002 P&OSL Canterbury, 2002-2004 PO Canterbury, 2004-2004 Alkmini A
Year of construction	1980

Call sign	C6TY9	**Classification**	Det Norske Veritas
IMO Number	7814462	**MMSI Number**	311852000
Length	163.96 m	**Gross tonnage**	25,318 GT
Beam	27.63 m	**Net tonnage**	12,889 NT
Draught	6.505 m	**Deadweight**	3,501 tdw
Passengers / Berths	1,000 / 480	**Maximum speed**	18 kn
Vehicles	500 Cars	**Cargo capacity**	1,765 lm or 66 Trailers

Main engines	2 x Sulzer 7 RLA 56, Diesel / each 6,510 kW
Auxiliary engines	3 x Diesel / each 3,000 kW
Propeller	2 x Propeller, controllable pitch
Bow thruster	2 x Tunnel / each 1,720 kW

▼ Scandlines

Scandlines can look back on a short but eventful history. Following the reunification of Germany the two German railway companies merged on January 1, 1994. The ferry lines, operated by the two companies, have been combined to the Deutschen Fährgesellschaft Ostsee mbH (DFO). In 1995 the Danish State Railways hived off their ferry company under the name DSB Rederi A/S and renamed it 1997 in Scandlines A/S. On July 21, 1998, the DFO and the Scandlines A/S merged to Scandlines AG. Owners remained the German Bahn AG and the Kingdom of Denmark until 2007, when the financial investor 3i and Allianz Capital Partners (ACP) each with 40% and the Deutsche Seereederei GmbH (DSR) took over the remaining 20% of the company shares. On November 6, 2008, Scandlines AG was transformed into a limited company and since then has been carrying the business name Scandlines GmbH, based in Rostock. The subsidiaries of Scandlines GmbH are Scandlines Germany Gmbh, based in Rostock and Scandlines Denmark A/S , based in Copenhagen.[28]In October 2010,the DSR sold its 20% stake to 3i and ACP. In 2013 ACP sold its shares to 3i, who became the sole owner of Scandlines. [29]

Figure 121: M/S Prinsesse Benedikte

Photo: © Scandlines

Figure 122: M/S Aurora af Helsingborg   Photo: © Stena Line

Name of ship   M/S Aurora af Helsingborg

Home port / Flag state	Helsingborg / Sweden
Shipyard / Yard number	Tangen Verft A/S, Kragerö, Norway / #100 / Langsten Slip & Båtbyggeri A/S, Tomrefjorden, Norway / #157
Previous ship names	-
Year of construction	1992

Call sign	SCQX	**Classification**	Lloyd´s Register of Shipping
IMO Number	9007128	**MMSI Number**	265041000
Length	111.20 m	**Gross tonnage**	10,845 GT
Beam (incl. fender)	28.20 m	**Net tonnage**	3,253 NT
Draught	5.50 m	**Deadweight**	2,547 tdw
Passengers	1,250	**Service speed**	14.5 kn
Vehicles	260 Cars	**Cargo capacity**	539 lm

Main engines	4 x Wärtsilä GR32E, 9,840 kW
Auxiliary engines	Unspecified
Propeller	4 x Propeller nacelles, swiveling
Bow thruster	Without, Function taken over by Propeller nacelles

Figure 123: M/S Berlin   Photo: © Patrick Kirkby / Wikimedia Commons CC-BY 3.0

Name of ship   M/S Berlin

Home port / Flag state   Rostock / Germany

Shipyard / Yard number   P+S Werften Stralsund, Germany / Fayard, Munkebo, Denmark / #502

Previous ship names   -

Year of construction   2016

Call sign	DKDF2	Classification	Lloyd's Register of Shipping
IMO Number	9587855	MMSI Number	218780000
Length	169.50 m	Gross tonnage	22,319 GT
Beam	24.80 m	Net tonnage	6,695 NT
Draught	5.5 m	Deadweight	4,200 tdw
Passengers	1,300	Service speed	22.5 kn
Vehicles	460 Cars	Cargo capacity	1,600 lm

Main engines   4 x Caterpillar 9M32CCR, Diesel / 15,800 kW

Auxiliary engines   Unspecified

Propeller   2 x Propeller, controllable pitch

Bow thruster   2 x Tunnel

Figure 124: M/S Copenhagen in Warnemuende   Photo: © Bernd Wuestneck / Wikimedia Commons CC-BY 3.0

Name of ship	M/S Copenhagen	

Home port / Flag state	Gedser / Denmark
Shipyard / Yard number	P+S Werften Stralsund, Germany / Fayard, Munkebo, Denmark / #503
Previous ship names	-
Year of construction	2016

Call sign	OXML2	**Classification**	Lloyd´s Register of Shipping
IMO Number	9587867	**MMSI Number**	219423000
Length	169.50 m	**Gross tonnage**	22,319 GT
Beam	24.80 m	**Net tonnage**	6,695 NT
Draught	5.5 m	**Deadweight**	4,200 tdw
Passengers	1,300	**Service speed**	22.5 kn
Vehicles	460 Cars	**Cargo capacity**	1,600 lm

Main engines	4 x Caterpillar 9M32CCR, Diesel / 15,800 kW
Auxiliary engines	Unspecified
Propeller	2 x Propeller, controllable pitch
Bow thruster	2 x Tunnel

Figure 125: M/S Deutschland

Photo: © Scandlines

Name of ship — M/S Deutschland

Home port / Flag state	Puttgarden / Germany
Shipyard / Yard number	Van der Giessen de Noord,Krimpen aan de Ijssel, Netherlands / #970
Previous ship names	-
Year of construction	1997

Call sign	DMLQ	**Classification**	Lloyd's Register of Shipping
IMO Number	9151541	**MMSI Number**	211188000
Length	142.00 m	**Gross tonnage**	15,187 GT
Beam (incl. fender)	25.40 m	**Net tonnage**	4,556 NT
Draught	5.80 m	**Deadweight**	2,904 tdw
Passengers	1,200	**Service speed**	18.5 kn
Vehicles	364 Cars	**Cargo capacity**	625 lm + 118 m Railway

Main engines	3 x MAK 8M32, Diesel / 15,840 kW
Auxiliary engines	2 x MAK 6M32, Diesel
Propeller	4 x Aquamaster KaMeWa, counterwise (2 x Starboard, 2 x Port)
Bow thruster	unspecified

Figure 126: M/S Hamlet   Photo: © Scandlines

Name of ship	M/S Hamlet	

Home port / Flag state   Helsingør / Denmark

Shipyard / Yard number   Finnyards, Rauma, Finland / #412

Previous ship names   -

Year of construction   1997

Call sign	OZMH2	Classification	Lloyd's Register of Shipping
IMO Number	9150030	MMSI Number	219622000
Length	111.20 m	Gross tonnage	10,067 GT
Beam (incl. fender)	28.20 m	Net tonnage	3,020 NT
Draught	5.30 m	Deadweight	2,860 tdw
Passengers	1,000	Service speed	13.5 kn
Vehicles	244 Cars	Cargo capacity	553 lm

Main engines   4 x Wärtsilä WDV 9L20, Diesel / 6,120 kW

Auxiliary engines   3 x Mitsubishi, S 6 R - MPTA 140 112

Propeller   4 x Propeller nacelles, swiveling

Bow thruster   Without, Function taken over by propeller nacelles

Figure 127: M/S Kronprins Frederik

Name of ship	M/S Kronprins Frederik

Home port / Flag state	Korsør / Denmark
Shipyard / Yard number	Nakskov Skibsværft A/S, Nakskov, Denmark / #224
Previous ship names	-
Year of construction	1981

Call sign	OYEM2	Classification	Lloyd's Register of Shipping
IMO Number	7803205	MMSI Number	219000479
Length	152.00 m	Gross tonnage	16,071 GT
Beam	23.70 m	Net tonnage	4,821 NT
Draught	5.30 m	Deadweight	2,726 tdw
Passengers	1,082	Service speed	20.5 kn
Vehicles	210 Cars	Cargo capacity	700 lm

Main engines	4 x MAK 8M32C, Diesel / 16,000 kW
Auxiliary engines	2 x MAK 6M32, Diesel
Propeller	2 x Propeller, controllable pitch
Bow thruster	2 x KaMeWa , Tunnel

Figure 128: M/S Prinsesse Benedikte   Photo: © Scandlines

| Name of ship | M/S Prinsesse Benedikte | |

Home port / Flag state   Rødbyhavn / Denmark

Shipyard / Yard number   Ørskov Staalskibsværft, Frederikshavn, Denmark / #194

Previous ship names   -

Year of construction   1997

Call sign	OYDX2	Classification	Lloyd´s Register of Shipping
IMO Number	9144421	MMSI Number	219000431
Length	142.00 m	Gross tonnage	14,822 GT
Beam	25.40 m	Net tonnage	4,446 NT
Draught	5.82 m	Deadweight	2,248 tdw
Passengers	1,140	Service speed	18.5 kn
Vehicles	364 Cars	Cargo capacity	1,747 lm Cars, 580 lm Lorries

Main engines   4 x MAK 8M32, Diesel / 14,080 kW

Auxiliary engines   1 x MAN 6L32 / 44CR, Diesel

Propeller   4 x Aquamaster KaMeWa Propeller nacelles

Bow thruster   2 x Tunnel

Figure 129: M/S Prins Richard   Photo: © Scandlines

Name of ship   M/S Prins Richard

Home port / Flag state	Rødbyhavn / Denmark
Shipyard / Yard number	Ørskov Christensen Staalskibsværft A/S, Frederikshavn, Denmark / #193
Previous ship names	-
Year of construction	1997

Call sign	OZLB2	**Classification**	Lloyd's Register of Shipping
IMO Number	9144419	**MMSI Number**	219000429
Length	142.00 m	**Gross tonnage**	14,822 GT
Beam (incl. fender)	25.40 m	**Net tonnage**	4,446 NT
Draught	5.82 m	**Deadweight**	2,230 tdw
Passengers	1,140	**Service speed**	18.5 kn
Vehicles	364 Cars	**Cargo capacity**	580 lm, 118m Railway

Main engines	5 x MAK 8M32C, Diesel / 14,080 kW
Auxiliary engines	2 x MAK 6M32, Diesel
Propeller	4 x Aquamaster KaMeWa Propeller nacelles, swiveling
Bow thruster	Without, Function taken over by Propeller nacelles

Figure 130: M/S Schleswig-Holstein   Photo: © Scandlines

Name of ship	M/S Schleswig-Holstein

Home port / Flag state	Puttgarden / Germany
Shipyard / Yard number	Van der Giessen de Noord,Krimpen aan de Ijssel, Netherlands / #969
Previous ship names	-
Year of construction	1997

Call sign	DMLM	**Classification**	Lloyd's Register of Shipping
IMO Number	9151539	**MMSI Number**	211190000
Length	142.00 m	**Gross tonnage**	15,187 GT
Beam (incl. fender)	25.40 m	**Net tonnage**	4,556 NT
Draught	5.80 m	**Deadweight**	2,904 tdw
Passengers	1,200	**Service speed**	18.5 kn
Vehicles	364 Cars	**Cargo capacity**	625 lm + 118 m Railway

Main engines	3 x MAK 8M32, Diesel / 10,560 kW
Auxiliary engines	2 x MAK 6M32, Diesel
Propeller	4 x Aquamaster KaMeWa, counterwise (2 x Starboard, 2 x Port)
Bow thruster	Unspecified

Figure 131: M/S Tycho Brahe   Photo: © Schummchen / Wikimedia Commons CC BY-SA 3.0

Name of ship	M/S Tycho Brahe	

Home port / Flag state	Helsingør / Denmark
Shipyard / Yard number	Tangen Verft A/S, Kragerö, Norway / #99 / Langsten Slip & Båtbyggeri A/S, Tomrefjorden, Norway / #156
Previous ship names	-
Year of construction	1991

Call sign	OVIC2	Classification	Lloyd's Register of Shipping
IMO Number	9007116	**MMSI Number**	219230000
Length	111.20 m	**Gross tonnage**	11,233 GT
Beam (incl. fender)	28.20 m	**Net tonnage**	3,344 NT
Draught	5.50 m	**Deadweight**	2,833 tdw
Passengers	1,250	**Service speed**	14.5 kn
Vehicles	240 Cars	**Cargo capacity**	539 lm

Main engines	4 x Wärtsilä 6R32E, 9,840 kW
Auxiliary engines	Unspecified
Propeller	4 x Propeller nacelles, swiveling
Bow thruster	Without, Function taken over by propeller nacelles

Figure 132: M/S Norröna / Route   Photo: © Smyril Line

Smyril Line  (Faroe Islands)

Smyril Line was founded in 1982 with the aim to connect the countries in the North Atlantic, including the Faroe Islands, Iceland and Denmark together. Smyril-Line has only one ship - the M/S Norröna. The ship offers a year-round service between Denmark and the Faroe Islands, during the period from April until October the trip goes until Iceland one time per week. Smyril Line is headquartered in Torshavn / Faroe Islands, and owns other booking offices in Hirtshals (Denmark), in Reykjavik (Iceland) as well as in Kiel (Germany). Furthermore, general agencies exist in Sweden, Finland, Belgium, Netherlands, France and Italy. [30]

Figure 133: Smyril Line headquarter in Torshavn   Photo: © Smyril Line

Figure 134: M/S Norröna

Photo: © Smyril Line

Name of ship — M/S Norröna

Home port / Flag state	Torshavn / Faroe Islands
Shipyard / Yard number	Flendern Werft AG, Lübeck, Germany / #694
Previous ship names	-
Year of construction	2003

Call sign	OZ2040	Classification	Det Norske Veritas
IMO Number	9227390	MMSI Number	231200000
Length	161.00 m	Gross tonnage	35,966 GT
Beam	33.50 m	Net tonnage	15,922 NT
Draught	6.00 m	Deadweight	6,113 tdw
Passengers / Cabins	1,482 / 318	Maximum speed	21 kn
Vehicles	800 Cars	Cargo capacity	130 Trailers, 1,830 lm or 3,250 t

Main engines	4 x Caterpillar MAK 6M43, Diesel / 21,600 kW
Auxiliary engines	3 x Caterpillar 9M20, Diesel
Propeller	2 x Propeller, controllable pitch Schottel
Bow thruster	2 x Brunvoll FU 100 LTC 2750, Tunnel

Figure 135: Stena Germanica II and III in the ferry port of Göteborg (Sweden)

Stena Line was founded in 1962 by Sten Allan Olsson, when he took over the Swedish ferry company Skagenlinjen . This was accompanied by the acquisition of the route Gothenburg - Nordjylland. In 1967 Stena was expanding its network with a new ferry service from Gothenburg to Kiel, and in 1979 from Frederikshavn, Denmark to Oslo. Stena Line since 1983 consistently expanded its business Travels, Hotels, Conferences on board and coach tours. To fund further international expansion, in 1987 half of the Stena shares were sold and the company became listed in the following year on the Stockholm Stock Exchange for the first time. 1990 Stena Line expanded greatly and doubled its size with the acquisition of Sealink British Ferries and some smaller Dutch shipping companies. With these aquisitions Stena Line became one of the largest ferry companies in the world. To be able to compete with the new opened Euro Tunnel, Stena Line decided in 1998 to form a joint venture with P&O Line on the routes Calais-Dover and Zeebrugge-Dover. Thus, the P & O Stena Line was born. The year 2000 brought a further expansion through the acquisition of the Swedish Stena Line AB Öresund with 4 new routes between Denmark and Sweden and between Sweden and Germany. In the following year, Stena Line went back to be a 100% privately-owned and withdrew from the Stockholm Stock Exchange. From now on, Stena Line was subsidiary of Stena AB. In 2002 Stena Line sold it's 40% stake in the joint venture P&O Stena Line to P&O and closed with this step the chapter of the collaboration with P&O. [31]

Figure 136: M/S Mecklenburg-Vorpommern   Photo: © Stena Line Trelleborg

Name of ship M/S Mecklenburg-Vorpommern

Home port / Flag state   Rostock / Germany

Shipyard / Yard number   Schichau Seebeckswerft AG, Bremerhaven, Germany / #1092

Previous ship names   -

Year of construction   1996

Call sign	DQLV	Classification	Lloyd's Register of Shipping
IMO Number	913179	MMSI Number	211245200
Length	199,98 m	Gross tonnage	37,987 GT
Beam	28.95 m	Net tonnage	11,623 NT
Draught	6.20 m	Deadweight	8,920 tdw
Passengers / Cabins	600 / 161	Maximum speed	22.5 kn
Vehicles	445 Cars	Cargo capacity	3,198 lm, thereof 945 lm Railway

Main engines   4x MAN B+W 6L48/60, Diesel / 25,200 kW

Propeller   2 x Propeller, controllable pitch

Bow thruster   2 x Tunnel

Figure 137: M/S Sassnitz   Photo: © Christian Kowalski / Stena Line

Name of ship   M/S Sassnitz

Home port / Flag state	Sassnitz / Germany
Shipyard / Yard number	Danyard A/S, Aalborg, Frederikshavn Værft A/S, Frederikshavn, Denmark / #690
Previous ship names	-
Year of construction	1989

Call sign	DQEJ	Classification	Lloyd´s Register of Shipping
IMO Number	8705383	**MMSI Number**	211189000
Length	171.50 m	**Gross tonnage**	21,154 GT
Beam	24.05 m	**Net tonnage**	7,192 NT
Draught	4.80 m	**Deadweight**	5,050 tdw
Passengers / Cabins	875 / 56	**Maximum speed**	20 kn
Vehicles	314 Cars	**Cargo capacity**	1,235 lm for Lorries

Main engines	2 x MAN-B&W 8L40/54, Diesel, 18,200 kW
Auxiliary engines	2 x MAN-B&W 6L40/54, Diesel
Propeller	2 x Propeller, controllable pitch EG135
Bow thruster	2 x Tunnel

Figure 138: M/S Scottish Viking   Photo: © Tim Becker / Stena Line

Name of ship — M/S Scottish Viking

Home port / Flag state	Bari / Italy
Shipyard / Yard number	C.N. "Visentini" di Visentini Francesco & C, Porto Viro, Italy / #221
Previous ship names	-
Year of construction	2009

Call sign	IBDZ	Classification	Registro Italiano Navale
IMO Number	9435454	**MMSI Number**	247265800
Length	186.00 m	**Gross tonnage**	26,904 GT
Beam	25.60 m	**Net tonnage**	9,000 NT
Draught	6.85 m	**Deadweight**	7,000 tdw
Passengers	852	**Maximum speed**	24 kn
Vehicles	195 Cars	**Cargo capacity**	2,250 lm

Main engines	2 x MAN B&W 9L48/60B, Diesel, 21,600 kW
Auxiliary engines	3 x Diesel / 5,703 kW
Propeller	2 x Propeller, controllable pitch
Bow thruster	2 x Tunnel

Figure 139: M/S Skåne   Photo: © Stena Line

Name of ship	M/S Skåne	

Home port / Flag state	Trelleborg / Sweden
Shipyard / Yard number	Puerto Real Astilleros Espanoles SRL, Spain / #77
Previous ship names	-
Year of construction	1998

Call sign	SIEB	Classification	Lloyd's Register of Shipping
IMO Number	9133915	**MMSI Number**	265463000
Length	200.20 m	**Gross tonnage**	42,705 GT
Beam	29.00 m	**Net tonnage**	21,731 NT
Draught	6.50 m	**Deadweight**	7,290 tdw
Passengers / Cabins	600 / 600	**Maximum speed**	21 kn
Vehicles	500 Cars	**Cargo capacity**	3,295 lm Vehicles / 1,110 lm Railway

Main engines	4 x MAN B&W 8L48/60 / 28,960 kW
Auxiliary engines	Unspecified
Propeller	2 x Propeller, controllable pitch
Bow thruster	3 x Tunnel

Figure 140: M/S Stena Baltica   Photo: © Lukasz Blaszczak / Stena Line

Name of ship	M/S Stena Baltica	

Home port / Flag state	London / United Kingdom
Shipyard / Yard number	Aker Yards Oy, Rauma, Finland / #1357
Previous ship names	2007-2013 Cotentin
Year of construction	2007

Call sign	2HAL4	**Classification**	Bureau Veritas
IMO Number	9364978	**MMSI Number**	235102029
Length	165.00 m	**Gross tonnage**	22,308 GT
Beam	26.80 m	**Net tonnage**	6,692 NT
Draught	6.50 m	**Deadweight**	6,200 tdw
Passengers / Berths	216 / 216	**Maximum speed**	23 kn
Vehicles	100 Cars	**Cargo capacity**	2,188 lm or 120 Lorries

Main engines	2 x MAK 12M43C, Diesel / 24,000 kW
Auxiliary engines	2 x Diesel / 1,386 kW
Propeller	2 x Propeller, controllable pitch LB 10.00
Bow thruster	2 x Tunnel

Figure 141: M/S Stena Britannica   Photo: © Stena Line

Name of ship   M/S Stena Britannica

Home port / Flag state	London / United Kingdom
Shipyard / Yard number	Wadan Yards MTW GmbH, Wismar, Germany / #164
Previous ship names	-
Year of construction	2010

Call sign	2DMO6	Classification	Lloyd´s Register of Shipping
IMO Number	9419175	MMSI Number	235080274
Length	240.87 m	Gross tonnage	64,039 GT
Beam	32.00 m	Net tonnage	36,870 NT
Draught	6.50 m	Deadweight	11,600 tdw
Passengers / Cabins	1,200 / 540	Maximum speed	22 kn
Vehicles	230 Cars	Cargo capacity	5,500 lm or 300 Lorries

Main engines	2 x MAN 8L48/60CR, Diesel, each 9,600 kW, 2 x MAN 6L48/60CR, Diesel, each 7,200 kW
Auxiliary engines	Unspecified
Propeller	2 x Propeller, controllable pitch
Bow thruster	2 x Tunnel

Figure 142: HSC Stena Carisma

Photo: © Jonas Carlsson / Stena Line

Name of ship   HSC Stena Carisma

Home port / Flag state	Göteborg / Sweden
Shipyard / Yard number	Westamarin A/S, Mandal, Norway / #238
Previous ship names	-
Year of construction	1997

Call sign	SGFV	**Classification**	Det Norske Veritas
IMO Number	9127760	**MMSI Number**	265430000
Length	89.75 m	**Gross tonnage**	8,631 GT
Beam	30.47 m	**Net tonnage**	2,589 NT
Draught	3.90 m	**Deadweight**	480 tdw
Passengers	900	**Maximum speed**	38 kn
Vehicles	210 Cars or 151 Cars + 10 Lorries	**Cargo capacity**	Unspecified

Main engines	2 x ABB-GT35 Gas turbines, 34,000 kW
Auxiliary engines	4 × MTU 12V 183 TE52, Diesel / 2,080 kW
Propeller	2 x KaMeWa Waterjet
Bow thruster	2 x KaMeWa 900 CRP-FP, Tunnel

Figure 143: M/S Stena Danica   Photo: © Bo Randstedt / Wikimedia Commons CC-BY-SA-3.0

Name of ship	M/S Stena Danica	

Home port / Flag state	Göteborg / Sweden
Shipyard / Yard number	Chantiers du Nord et de la Méditerranée, Dunkerque, France / #309
Previous ship names	-
Year of construction	1983

Call sign	SKFH	Classification	Det Norske Veritas
IMO Number	7907245	MMSI Number	265177000
Length	154.89 m	Gross tonnage	28,727 GT
Beam	28.04 m	Net tonnage	8,700 NT
Draught	6.317 m	Deadweight	2,950 tdw
Passengers / Cabins	2,274 / 96	Maximum speed	21 kn
Vehicles	550 Cars	Cargo capacity	1,806 lm

Main engines	4 x Sulzer 12ZV 40/48, Diesel / 25,743 kW
Auxiliary engines	5 x Sulzer 6ASL 25/30, Diesel
Propeller	2 x Propeller, controllable pitch Lips RO 600
Bow thruster	2 x Lips CT 16 H, Tunnel

Figure 144: M/S Stena Flavia   Photo: © Krists Afanasjevs / Stena Line

Name of ship	M/S Stena Flavia	

Home port / Flag state	Frederikshavn / Denmark
Shipyard / Yard number	Cantiere Navale Visentini, Porto Viro, Italy / #219
Previous ship names	2008-2008 Watling Street 2008-2010 Pilar del Mar 2010-2013 Watling Street
Year of construction	2008

Call sign	2ASI7	Classification	Registro Italiano Navale
IMO Number	9417919	**MMSI Number**	235064391
Length	186.00 m	**Gross tonnage**	26,904 GT
Beam	25.60 m	**Net tonnage**	9,000 NT
Draught	6.85 m	**Deadweight**	7,000 tdw
Passengers	852	**Maximum speed**	24 kn
Vehicles	195 Cars	**Cargo capacity**	2,250 lm

Main engines	2 x MAN B&W 9L48/60B, Diesel / 21,600 kW
Auxiliary engines	4 x Diesel / 6,113 kW
Propeller	2 x Propeller, controllable pitch
Bow thruster	2 x Tunnel

Figure 145: M/S Stena Germanica   Photo: © Stena Line

Name of ship   M/S Stena Germanica

Home port / Flag state	Göteborg / Sweden
Shipyard / Yard number	Astilleros Españoles, Puerta Real, Spain / #81
Previous ship names	2001-2010 Stena Hollandica, 2010 Stena Germanica III
Year of construction	2001

Call sign	SLDW	**Classification**	Lloyd's Register of Shipping
IMO Number	9145176	**MMSI Number**	266331000
Length	241.26 m	**Gross tonnage**	51,837 GT
Beam	28.70 m	**Net tonnage**	17,209 NT
Draught	6.30 m	**Deadweight**	10,670 tdw
Passengers / Berths	1,200 / 1,200	**Maximum speed**	22 kn
Vehicles	300 Cars	**Cargo capacity**	4,000 lm

Main engines	4 x Sulzer 8ZAL40S, Diesel / Methanol, 24,000 kW
Auxiliary engines	Unspecified
Propeller	2 x Propeller, controllable pitch
Bow thruster	2 x Tunnel

Figure 146: M/S Stena Gothica   Photo: © Bo Randstedt / Wikimedia Commons CC BY-SA 3.0

Name of ship   M/S Stena Gothica

Home port / Flag state	Göteborg / Sweden
Shipyard / Yard number	Nuovi Cantieri Aquania SpA. ,Marina, Italy / #2120
Previous ship names	1982-1984 Lucky Rider, 1984-1985 Stena Driver, 1985-1988 Seafreight Freeway, 1988-1990 Serdica, 1990-1991 Nordic Hunter, 1991-1991 Arka Marine, 1991-2015 Ask
Year of construction	1982

Call sign	OUVU2	**Classification**	Lloyd's Register of Shipping
IMO Number	7826867	**MMSI Number**	219000627
Length	171.06 m	**Gross tonnage**	13,294 GT
Beam	20.20 m	**Net tonnage**	2,406 NT
Draught	5.27 m	**Deadweight**	4,550 tdw
Passengers / Cabins	548 / 52	**Maximum speed**	17.5 kn
Vehicles	291 Cars	**Cargo capacity**	1070 lm + 69 Trailers

Main engines	2 x Wärtsilä-Vasa 12 V32E / Diesel / 9,840 kW
Propeller	2 x Propeller, controllable pitch
Bow thruster	3 x Tunnel

Figure 147: M/S Stena Hollandica   Photo: © Stena Line

Name of ship   M/S Stena Hollandica

Home port / Flag state   Hoek van Holland / Netherlands

Shipyard / Yard number   Wadan Yards MTW GmbH, Wismar, Germany / #159

Previous ship names   -

Year of construction   2010

Call sign	PBMM	Classification	Lloyd's Register of Shipping
IMO Number	9419163	MMSI Number	244758000
Length	240.87 m	Gross tonnage	64,039 GT
Beam	32.00 m	Net tonnage	36,870 NT
Draught	6.50 m	Deadweight	11,600 tdw
Passengers / Cabins	1,200 / 540	Maximum speed	22 kn
Vehicles	230 Cars	Cargo capacity	5,500 lm or 300 Lorries

Main engines   2 x MAN 8L48/60CR, Diesel / each 9,600 kW,
                        2 x MAN 6L48/60CR, Diesel / each 7,200 kW

Auxiliary engines   Unspecified

Propeller   2 x Propeller, controllable pitch

Bow thruster   2 x Tunnel

Figure 148: M/S Stena Horizon   Photo: © Stena Line

Name of ship   M/S Stena Horizon

Home port / Flag state	Bari / Italy
Shipyard / Yard number	Cantieri Navale Visentini, Portoviro, Italy / #214
Previous ship names	2006-2011 Cartour Beta 2011-2014 Celtic Horizon
Year of construction	2006

Call sign	IBPT	Classification	Registro Italiano Navale
IMO Number	9332559	**MMSI Number**	247160400
Length	177.40 m	**Gross tonnage**	27,522 GT
Beam	25.60 m	**Net tonnage**	Unspecified
Draught	6.60 m	**Deadweight**	7,300 tdw
Passengers / Cabins	972 / 156	**Maximum speed**	24 kn
Vehicles	186 Cars	**Cargo capacity**	2,244 lm / 173 Lorries or Trailers

Main engines	2 x MAN 9L48/60B Diesel / 21,600 kW
Auxiliary engines	4 x 1,528 kW, Diesel
Propeller	2 x Propeller, controllable pitch
Bow thruster	2 x Tunnel / 1,300 kW

Figure 149: M/S Stena Jutlandica   Photo: © Stena Line

Name of ship	M/S Stena Jutlandica	

Home port / Flag state	Göteborg / Sweden
Shipyard / Yard number	Van der Gissen de Noord, Krimpen a/d, Ijssel, Netherlands / #967
Previous ship names	1996-1996 Stena Jutlandica III
Year of construction	1996

Call sign	SEAN	Classification	Lloyd's Register of Shipping
IMO Number	9125944	**MMSI Number**	265410000
Length	182.35 m	**Gross tonnage**	29,691 GT
Beam	27.80 m	**Net tonnage**	9,046 NT
Draught	6.00 m	**Deadweight**	6,559 tdw
Passengers / Cabins	1,200 / 200	**Maximum speed**	21.5 kn
Vehicles	550 Cars	**Cargo capacity**	600 lm or 122 Trailers

Main engines	4 x MAN B&W 9L48/54, Diesel / 25,920 kW
Auxiliary engines	Unspecified
Propeller	2 x Propeller, controllable pitch
Bow thruster	2 x Tunnel

Figure 150: M/S Stena Nautica

Photo: © Niklas Nolte / Stena Line

Name of ship — M/S Stena Nautica

Home port / Flag state	Göteborg / Sweden
Shipyard / Yard number	Nakskov Skibsvaerft A/S, Nakskov, Denmark / #234
Previous ship names	1986-1991 Niels Klim, 1991-1992 Stena Nautica, 1992-1995 Isle of Innisfree, 1995-1996 Lion King 1996-1996 Lion King II
Year of construction	1986

Call sign	SGQU	Classification	Lloyd's Register of Shipping
IMO Number	8317954	MMSI Number	265859000
Length	135.46 m	Gross tonnage	19,504 GT
Beam	24.00 m	Net tonnage	6,180 NT
Draught	5.84 m	Deadweight	3,676 tdw
Passengers / Cabins	900 / 148	Maximum speed	18 kn
Vehicles	324 Cars	Cargo capacity	1,235 lm

Main engines	2 x B&W 8L45GB, Diesel / 12,470 kW
Propeller	2 x Propeller, controllable pitch
Bow thruster	2 x Tunnel

Figure 151: M/S Stena Saga
Photo: © John Wilson / Stena Line

Name of ship · M/S Stena Saga

Home port / Flag state	Stockholm / Sweden
Shipyard / Yard number	Oy Wärtsilä AB, Perno und Åbo, Finland / #1252
Previous ship names	1981-1991 Silvia Regina, 1991-1994 Stena Britannica
Year of construction	1981

Call sign	SLVH	Classification	Lloyd's Register of Shipping
IMO Number	7911545	MMSI Number	265001000
Length	166.10 m	Gross tonnage	33,967 GT
Beam	29.06 m	Net tonnage	17,528 NT
Draught	6.70 m	Deadweight	3,898 tdw
Passengers / Berths	2,000 / 1,601	Maximum speed	22 kn
Vehicles	510 Cars	Cargo capacity	70 Trailers

Main engines	4 x Wärtsilä-Pielstick 12PC2,5V, Diesel / 22,948 kW
Auxiliary engines	Unspecified
Propeller	2 x Propeller, controllable pitch
Bow thruster	2 x Tunnel

Figure 152: M/S Stena Scandinavica   Photo: © Stena Line

Name of ship   M/S Stena Scandinavica

Home port / Flag state	Göteborg / Sweden
Shipyard / Yard number	Hyundai Heavy Industries, South Korea / #1392
Previous ship names	2003-2003 Stena Britannica II, 2003-2010 Britannica, 2010-2011 Stena Scandinavica IV
Year of construction	2003

Call sign	SJLB	**Classification**	Lloyd´s Register of Shipping
IMO Number	9235517	**MMSI Number**	266343000
Length	240.09 m	**Gross tonnage**	57,958 GT
Beam	29.30 m	**Net tonnage**	24,087 NT
Draught	6.314 m	**Deadweight**	12,200 tdw
Passengers / Berths	1,300 / 1,040	**Maximum speed**	22.5 kn
Vehicles	300 Cars	**Cargo capacity**	4,220 lm

Main engines	4 x MAN-B&W 9L40/54, Diesel / 25,920 kW
Auxiliary engines	Unspecified
Propeller	2 x Propeller, controllable pitch
Bow thruster	3 x Tunnel

Figure 153: M/S Stena Spirit

Photo: © Stena Line

Name of ship — M/S Stena Spirit

Home port / Flag state	Nassau / Bahamas
Shipyard / Yard number	Lenina Stocznia Gdanska, Gdansk, Poland / #B494/2
Previous ship names	1983-1986 Stena Germanica, 1986-2011 Stena Scandinavica
Year of construction	1983

Call sign	C6ZK8	**Classification**	Lloyd's Register of Shipping
IMO Number	7907661	**MMSI Number**	311058100
Length	175.39 m	**Gross tonnage**	39,193 GT
Beam	30.46 m	**Net tonnage**	22,089 NT
Draught	6.701 m	**Deadweight**	4,500 tdw
Passengers / Berths	1,700 / 1,700	**Maximum speed**	21.5 kn
Vehicles	569 Cars	**Cargo capacity**	1,628 lm

Main engines	4 x Zgoda-Sulzer 16ZV49/48, Diesel / #33,098 kW
Auxiliary engines	Unspecified
Propeller	2 x Propeller, controllable pitch
Bow thruster	2 x Tunnel

Figure 154: M/S Stena Transit   Photo: © Ghega / Wikimedia Commons CC BY-SA 3.0

Name of ship — M/S Stena Transit

Home port / Flag state	Hoek van Holland / Netherlands
Shipyard / Yard number	Samsung Heavy Industries Co., Ltd., Hwaseong, South Korea / #1808
Previous ship names	-
Year of construction	2011

Call sign	PHJU	**Classification**	Lloyd's Register of Shipping
IMO Number	9469388	**MMSI Number**	244513000
Length	212.00 m	**Gross tonnage**	33,690 GT
Beam	31.62 m	**Net tonnage**	17,330 NT
Draught	6.30 m	**Deadweight**	8,420 tdw
Passengers / Berths	300 / 256	**Maximum speed**	22 kn
Vehicles	Unspecified	**Cargo capacity**	4,057 lm

Main engines	2 x STX-MAN 9L 48/60 B, Diesel / each 10,800 kW
Auxiliary engines	Unspecified
Propeller	2 x Propeller, controllable pitch
Bow thruster	2 x Tunnel

Figure 155: M/S Stena Transporter

Name of ship   M/S Stena Transporter

Home port / Flag state	Hoek van Holland / Netherlands
Shipyard / Yard number	Samsung Heavy Industries, Hwaseong, South Korea / #1807
Previous ship names	-
Year of construction	2011

Call sign	PCIY	**Classification**	Lloyd's Register of Shipping
IMO Number	9469376	**MMSI Number**	246762000
Length	212.00 m	**Gross tonnage**	33,690 GT
Beam	31.62 m	**Net tonnage**	17,330 NT
Draught	6.30 m	**Deadweight**	8,423 tdw
Passengers / Berths	300 / 256	**Maximum speed**	22 kn
Vehicles	Unspecified	**Cargo capacity**	4,057 lm

Main engines	2 x STX-MAN 9L 48/60 B, Diesel / each 10,800 kW
Auxiliary engines	Unspecified
Propeller	2 x Propeller, controllable pitch
Bow thruster	2 x Tunnel

Figure 156: M/S Stena Vision   Photo: © Stena Line

Name of ship	M/S Stena Vision

Home port / Flag state	Karlskrona / Sweden
Shipyard / Yard number	Stocnia i Komuni Paryski, Gdynia, Poland / #B494/1
Previous ship names	1981-1982 Stena Scandinavica, 1982-1986 Scandinavica, 1986-2010 Stena Germanica
Year of construction	1981

Call sign	SKPZ	Classification	Lloyd's Register of Shipping
IMO Number	7907659	MMSI Number	265292000
Length	175.37 m	Gross tonnage	39,191 GT
Beam	30.46 m	Net tonnage	22,089 NT
Draught	6.701 m	Deadweight	4,500 tdw
Passengers / Berths	1,700 / 1700	Maximum speed	21.5 kn
Vehicles	569 Cars	Cargo capacity	1,628 lm

Main engines	4 x Zgoda-Sulzer 16ZV49/48, Diesel / 33,098 kW
Auxiliary engines	Unspecified
Propeller	2 x Propeller, controllable pitch
Bow thruster	2 x Tunnel

Figure 157: M/S Urd   Photo: © Stena Line

Name of ship	M/S Urd	

Home port / Flag state	Kalundborg / Denmark
Shipyard / Yard number	Nuovi Cantieri Aquania SpA, Marina, Italy / #2119
Previous ship names	1981-1987 Easy Rider, 1987-1988 Seafreight Highway, 1988-1990 Boyana, 1990-1991 AktivMarine
Year of construction	1981

Call sign	OUYL2	**Classification**	Lloyd's Register of Shipping
IMO Number	7826855	**MMSI Number**	219000776
Length	171,05 m	**Gross tonnage**	13,144 GT
Beam	20.21 m	**Net tonnage**	3,309 NT
Draught	5.19 m	**Deadweight**	4,562 tdw
Passengers / Berths	600 / 105	**Maximum speed**	17.3 kn
Vehicles	325 Cars	**Cargo capacity**	1,600 lm

Main engines	2 x Wärtsilä-Vasa 12V32E / Diesel / 9,708 kW
Auxiliary engines	Unspecified
Propeller	2 x Propeller, controllable pitch
Bow thruster	3 x Tunnel

TALLINK SILJA LINE

In 1883 Finska Ångfartygs Ab - Suomen Höyrylaiva Oy (Finnish steamship AB) was founded, which merged in 1957 with the Swedish Stockholms Rederi Ab Svea and the Finnish Ångfartygs from Bore, Turku to form the shipping company Siljarederiet -Siljavarustamo. The management of the shipping company Silja recognized early enough the future importance of the Ro-Pax ferry traffic. In 1961 the first Finnish ferry was put into service with the Wärtsilä (Helsinki) built M/S Skandia . In 1999 the British Sea Containers Ltd. bought the majority of Silja and took over all the shares of Silja until 2002. 2006 Silja was sold to the Estonian AS Tallink Group.

After the acquisition of Silja by Tallink, 6 of the 11 Silja-ferries remained the property of Tallink, the rest remained at Sea Containers. After 2006 the Finnish subsidiaries of Tallink (Tallink Finland Oy ,Silja Oy Ab and Superfast Finland) merged under the umbrella of Silja Oy Ab, the name was changed to Tallink Silja Oy in December 2006. The headquarter of Tallink Silja Oy is until today located in Espoo (Finland). The Swedish sub-sidiaries were summarized as Tallink Silja AB, located in Stockholm. [32]

Figure 158: M/S Baltic Queen

Photo: © Magnus Rietz/Tallink Silja Oy

Figure 159: M/S Baltic Princess   Photo: © Hannu Nieminen / Tallink Silja Oy

Name of ship	M/S Baltic Princess	

Home port / Flag state	Mariehamn / Finland
Shipyard / Yard number	STX Finland Oy, Rauma, Finland / #1361
Previous ship names	-
Year of construction	2008

Call sign	OJQF	Classification	Bureau Veritas
IMO Number	9354284	MMSI Number	230639000
Length	212.10 m	Gross tonnage	48,915 GT
Beam	29.00 m	Net tonnage	30,860 NT
Draught	6.42 m	Deadweight	6,287 tdw
Passengers / Berths	2,800 / 2,500	Maximum speed	24.5 kn
Vehicles	420 Cars	Cargo capacity	1,130 lm

Main engines	4 × Wärtsilä 16V32, Diesel / 32,000 kW
Auxiliary engines	Unspecified
Propeller	2 x Propeller, controllable pitch LB 10.00
Bow thruster	2 x Tunnel

Figure 160: M/S Baltic Queen

Photo: © Tallink Silja Oy

Name of ship · M/S Baltic Queen

Home port / Flag state	Tallinn / Estonia
Shipyard / Yard number	STX Finland Oy, Rauma, Finland / #1365
Previous ship names	-
Year of construction	2009

Call sign	ESJJ	Classification	Bureau Veritas
IMO Number	9443255	MMSI Number	276779000
Length	212.10 m	Gross tonnage	48,915 GT
Beam	29.00 m	Net tonnage	30,860 NT
Draught	6.42 m	Deadweight	6,287 tdw
Passengers / Berths	2,800 / 2,500	Maximum speed	24.5 kn
Vehicles	420 Cars	Cargo capacity	1,130 lm

Main engines	4 × Wärtsilä 16V32, Diesel / 32,000 kW
Auxiliary engines	Unspecified
Propeller	2 x Propeller, controllable pitch LB 10.00
Bow thruster	2 x Tunnel

Figure 161: M/S Galaxy   Photo: © Marko Stampehl / Tallink Silja Oy

Name of ship	M/S Galaxy

Home port / Flag state	Stockholm / Sweden
Shipyard / Yard number	STX Finland Oy, Rauma, Finland / #435
Previous ship names	-
Year of construction	2006

Call sign	SFZQ	Classification	Bureau Veritas
IMO Number	9333694	MMSI Number	266301000
Length	212.10 m	Gross tonnage	48,915 GT
Beam	29.00 m	Net tonnage	30,860 NT
Draught	6.40 m	Deadweight	6,287 tdw
Passengers / Berths	2,700 / 2,200	Maximum speed	22 kn
Vehicles	420 Cars	Cargo capacity	1,130 lm

Main engines	4 x Wärtsilä, Diesel / 26,240 kW
Auxiliary engines	3 x Diesel / 2,360 kW
Propeller	2 x Propeller, controllable pitch LB 10.00
Bow thruster	2 x Tunnel

Figure 162: M/S Isabelle

Photo: © AS Tallink Grupp

Name of ship — M/S Isabelle

Home port / Flag state	Riga / Latvia
Shipyard / Yard number	Brodogradilište Split, Split, Croatia / #357
Previous ship names	1989-2013 Isabella
Year of construction	1989

Call sign	YLEZ	Classification	Det Norske Veritas
IMO Number	8700723	MMSI Number	275430000
Length	169.40 m	Gross tonnage	35,154 GT
Beam	28.20 m	Net tonnage	20,683 NT
Draught	6.418 m	Deadweight	3,680 tdw
Passengers / Berths	2,480 / 2,166	Maximum speed	21.5 kn
Vehicles	364 Cars	Cargo capacity	850 lm

Main engines	4 x Wärtsilä- Pielstick 12PC 2.6 2VE-400, Diesel / 24,000 kW
Auxiliary engines	4 x Wärtsilä 6R32 BC, Diesel
Propeller	2 x Propeller, controllable pitch KaMeWa 157XF3/4
Bow thruster	2 x KaMeWa 2400D/AS-CP, Tunnel

Figure 163: M/S Megastar   Photo: © AS Tallink Grupp

Name of ship   M/S Megastar

Home port / Flag state	Tallinn / Estonia
Shipyard / Yard number	Meyer Turku Oy, Åbo, Finland / #1391
Previous ship names	-
Year of construction	2017

Call sign	ESKL	Classification	Bureau Veritas
IMO Number	9773064	MMSI Number	276829000
Length	212.20 m	Gross tonnage	49,134 GT
Beam	30.60 m	Net tonnage	15,621 NT
Draught	7.10 m	Deadweight	6,300 tdw
Passengers	2,800	Maximum speed	27.0 kn
Vehicles	800 Cars	Cargo capacity	3,653 lm

Main engines	3 x Wärtsilä 12V50DF, Diesel/LNG / 40,600 kW
Auxiliary engines	2 x Wärtsilä 6L50DF, Diesel/LNG
Propeller	2 x Propeller, solid LB 10.00
Bow thruster	2 x Tunnel

Figure 164: M/S Romantika   Photo: © Magnus Rietz / Tallink Silja Oy

Name of ship — M/S Romantika

Home port / Flag state	Riga / Latvia
Shipyard / Yard number	Aker Finnyards, Rauma, Finland / #443
Previous ship names	-
Year of construction	2002

Call sign	YLBT	Classification	Lloyd's Register of Shipping
IMO Number	9237589	MMSI Number	275304000
Length	192.90 m	Gross tonnage	40,803 GT
Beam	29.00 m	Net tonnage	24,202 NT
Draught	6.50 m	Deadweight	4,500 tdw
Passengers / Cabins	2,500 / 727	Maximum speed	22 kn
Vehicles	300 Cars	Cargo capacity	1,030 lm

Main engines	4 x Wärtsilä 16V32 / Diesel / each 6,560 kW
Auxiliary engines	Unspecified
Propeller	2 x Propeller, controllable pitch
Bow thruster	2 x Tunnel

Figure 165: M/S Silja Europa   Photo: © Hannu Vallas / Tallink Silja Oy

Name of ship	M/S Silja Europa

Home port / Flag state	Tallinn / Estonia
Shipyard / Yard number	Meyer Werft GmbH, Papenburg, Germany / #627
Previous ship names	1993-1993 Europa
Year of construction	1993

Call sign	ESUJ	Classification	Bureau Veritas
IMO Number	8919805	MMSI Number	276807000
Length	201.80 m	Gross tonnage	59,914 GT
Beam	32.00 m	Net tonnage	41,309 NT
Draught	6.80 m	Deadweight	4,650 tdw
Passengers / Cabins	3,123 / 1,194	Maximum speed	21.5 kn
Vehicles	350 Cars	Cargo capacity	932 lm or 50 Lorries

Main engines	4 x MAN B&W 6L58/64, Diesel, 31,800 kW
Auxiliary engines	4 x Diesel, 2,245 kW
Propeller	2 x Propeller, controllable pitch LB 10.00
Bow thruster	4 x Tunnel

Figure 166: M/S Silja Serenade
Photo: © Magnus Rietz / Tallink Silja Oy

Name of ship — M/S Silja Serenade

Home port / Flag state	Mariehamn / Finland
Shipyard / Yard number	Masa-Yards Oy Turku , Åbo, Finland / #1301
Previous ship names	-
Year of construction	1990

Call sign	OJCS	**Classification**	Lloyd's Register of Shipping
IMO Number	8715259	**MMSI Number**	230184000
Length	203.03 m	**Gross tonnage**	58,376 GT
Beam	31.93 m	**Net tonnage**	35,961 NT
Draught	7.12 m	**Deadweight**	3,700 tdw
Passengers / Cabins	2,852 / 986	**Maximum speed**	21.5 kn
Vehicles	410 Cars	**Cargo capacity**	950 lm

Main engines	4 x Wärtsilä-Vasa 9R46 / Diesel / 32.580 kW
Auxiliary engines	Unspecified
Propeller	2 x Propeller, controllable pitch
Bow thruster	2 x Tunnel

Figure 167: M/S Silja Symphony   Photo: © AS Tallink Grupp

Name of ship	M/S Silja Symphony	

Home port / Flag state	Stockholm / Sweden
Shipyard / Yard number	Kvaerner Masa Yards, Turku, Finland / #1309
Previous ship names	-
Year of construction	1991

Call sign	SCGB	**Classification**	Lloyd´s Register of Shipping
IMO Number	8803769	**MMSI Number**	265004000
Length	203.03 m	**Gross tonnage**	58,377 GT
Beam	31.50 m	**Net tonnage**	35,962 NT
Draught	7.101 m	**Deadweight**	5,340 tdw
Passengers / Berths	2,852 / 2,700	**Maximum speed**	21 kn
Vehicles	410 Cars	**Cargo capacity**	950 lm

Main engines	4 × Wärtsilä-Vasa 9R46, Diesel / 32,500 kW
Auxiliary engines	Unspecified
Propeller	2 x Propeller, controllable pitch LB 10.00
Bow thruster	2 x Tunnel

Figure 168: M/S Star   Photo: © Hannu Vallas / Tallink Silja Oy

Name of ship	M/S Star	

Home port / Flag state	Tallinn / Estonia
Shipyard / Yard number	Aker Finnyards, Helsinki, Finland / #1356
Previous ship names	-
Year of construction	2007

Call sign	ESCJ	Classification	Bureau Veritas
IMO Number	9364722	MMSI Number	276672000
Length	186.00 m	Gross tonnage	36,249 GT
Beam	27.70 m	Net tonnage	13,316 NT
Draught	6.80 m	Deadweight	4,700 tdw
Passengers	1,900	Maximum speed	27.5 kn
Vehicles	450 Cars	Cargo capacity	2000 lm or 120 Lorries

Main engines	4 x MAK 12M43C / Diesel / 48,000 kW
Auxiliary engines	3 x Wärtsilä 8L20 / Diesel / 4,320 kW
Propeller	2 x Propeller, controllable pitch Wärtsilä
Bow thruster	2 x Wärtsilä / each 1,500 kW

Figure 169: M/S Victoria I   Photo: © AS Tallink Grupp

Name of ship   M/S Victoria I

Home port / Flag state	Tallinn / Estonia
Shipyard / Yard number	STX Finland Oy, Rauma, Finland / #434
Previous ship names	-
Year of construction	2004

Call sign	ESRP	Classification	Bureau Veritas
IMO Number	9281281	**MMSI Number**	276519000
Length	192.90 m	**Gross tonnage**	40,975 GT
Beam	29.00 m	**Net tonnage**	24,794 NT
Draught	6.60 m	**Deadweight**	4,930 tdw
Passengers / Berths	2,500 / 2,252	**Maximum speed**	22 kn
Vehicles	400 Cars	**Cargo capacity**	1,030 lm

Main engines	4 x Wärtsilä, Diesel / 26,240 kW
Auxiliary engines	2 x Diesel / 3,342 kW + 1 x Diesel / 1,984 kW
Propeller	2 x Propeller, controllable pitch LB 10.00
Bow thruster	2 x Tunnel

TT-Line

Figure 170: TT-Line headquarter "Hafenhaus" at Travemünde   Photo: © TT-Line

TT-Line was founded in 1962 by J.A.Reinecke as Travemünde-Trelleborg-Line (TT-Line). Later, the Trampschiffahrt GmbH & Co. KG and the Iduna - insurances took part in TT-Line. In 1967 the organizational structure of the shipping company was changed and from this time on named OHG Travemünde-Trelleborg-Linie & Co. In 1980, the German TT-Line founded, together with the Swedish Saga Linjen , a subsidiary of the Swedish State Railways , the TT- Saga Line. With a shared pool of six ships, the Swedish ports Trelleborg, Malmö and Helsingborg were connected with Travemünde . In 1982, the connections to Malmö and Helsingborg have been cancelled, and TT-Saga Line concentrated its activities on the route Travemünde-Trelleborg. 1991 Saga Linjen (now renamed Swedcarrier) withdrew from the pool. Their shares were acquired by the Swedish shipping company Gotlandsbolaget and at the end of 1992 again left the pool. So the German shareholders of TT-Line were the sole operators of the ferry service between Travemünde and Trelleborg. Together with the DSR Rostock GmbH TT-Line has operated since 1992 a ferry service between Trelleborg and Rostock under the name "TR-Line". In 1996, TT-Line took over the shares of DSR Rostock and served from then on the Rostock-Trelleborg route alone, now also under the brand name "TT-Line". Due to the strong increase in RO/RO traffic on the Baltic Sea the Skandinavienkai (Scandinavia wharf) was expanded in 2006 and a new terminal and office building, the Hafenhaus (Harbor house) was built. In August 2006, the corporate headquarters was moved from Hamburg to Lübeck-Travemünde. In 2013 Arend Oetker and Bernhard Termühlen took over (each of them 50 %) all the shares of TT-Line. [33]

Figure 171: M/S Huckleberry Finn   Photo: © TT-Line

Name of ship   M/S Huckleberry Finn

Home port / Flag state	Trelleborg / Sweden
Shipyard / Yard number	Schichau Seebeckswerft, Bremerhaven, Germany/ #1063
Previous ship names	1988-1993 Nils Dacke, 1993-2001 Peter Pan, 2001-2002 Peter Pan IV
Year of construction	1988

Call sign	SHLU	**Classification**	Germanischer Lloyd
IMO Number	8618358	**MMSI Number**	265874000
Length	177.20 m	**Gross tonnage**	26,391 GT
Beam	26.00 m	**Net tonnage**	8,417 NT
Draught	5.75 m	**Deadweight**	6,254 tdw
Passengers / Berths	400 / 324	**Maximum speed**	19 kn
Vehicles	535 Cars	**Cargo capacity**	2,240 lm on 3 Decks

Main engines	2 x MAN B&W 8L40/45 / Diesel / each 3,170 kW 2 x MAN B&W 6L40/45 / Diesel / each 4,230 kW
Auxiliary engines	4 x Diesel / each 1,025 kW
Propeller	2 x Propeller, controllable pitch
Bow thruster	2 x KaMeWa, Tunnel

Figure 172: M/S Nils Dacke   Photo: © TT-Line

Name of ship   M/S Nils Dacke

Home port / Flag state	Trelleborg / Sweden
Shipyard / Yard number	Finnyards Oy, Rauma, Finland / #411
Previous ship names	-
Year of construction	1995

Call sign	SFVP	**Classification**	Germanischer Lloyd
IMO Number	9087477	**MMSI Number**	266127000
Length	179.71 m	**Gross tonnage**	26,796 GT
Beam	27.20 m	**Net tonnage**	11,589 NT
Draught	6.00 m	**Deadweight**	6,538 tdw
Passengers / Berths	300 / 321	**Maximum speed**	19.5 kn
Vehicles	Unspecified	**Cargo capacity**	2,400 lm or 152 Lorries

Main engines	2 x MAK 6M552C, Diesel / each 6,500 kW
Auxiliary engines	4 x Diesel / each 4,500 kW
Propeller	2 x LIPS Fixed propeller
Bow thruster	2 x Tunnel / each 1,200 kW

Figure 173: M/S Nils Holgersson

Photo: © TT-Line

Name of ship	M/S Nils Holgersson	

Home port / Flag state	Lübeck / Germany
Shipyard / Yard number	SSW Fähr– und Spezialschiffbau GmbH, Bremerhaven, Germany / #2000
Previous ship names	-
Year of construction	2001

Call sign	DNPI	**Classification**	Germanischer Lloyd
IMO Number	9217230	**MMSI Number**	211343680
Length	190.77 m	**Gross tonnage**	36,468 GT
Beam	29.50 m	**Net tonnage**	10,940 NT
Draught	6.20 m	**Deadweight**	6,475 tdw
Passengers / Berths	744 / 640	**Maximum speed**	23 kn
Vehicles	Unspecified	**Cargo capacity**	174 Trailers on 2,640 lm on 3 Loading decks

Main engines	2 x SSP–Pods Diesel electric / each 11,000 kW 5 x Diesel generators / 29.880 kW
Propeller	4 x Rudder propeller
Bow thruster	2 x Brunvoll, Tunnel / each 2,400 kW

Figure 174: M/S Peter Pan   Photo: © TT-Line

Name of ship   M/S Peter Pan

Home port / Flag state	Trelleborg / Sweden
Shipyard / Yard number	SSW Fähr– und Spezialschiffbau GmbH, Bremerhaven, Germany / #2001
Previous ship names	-
Year of construction	2001

Call sign	SGUH	**Classification**	Germanischer Lloyd
IMO Number	9217242	**MMSI Number**	265866000
Length	190.77 m	**Gross tonnage**	36,468 GT
Beam	29.50 m	**Net tonnage**	10,940 NT
Draught	6.20 m	**Deadweight**	6,475 tdw
Passengers / Berths	744 / 640	**Maximum speed**	23 kn
Vehicles	Unspecified	**Cargo capacity**	174 Trailers on 2,640 lm on 3 Loading decks

Main engines	2 x SSP–Pods Diesel electric / each 11,000 kW 5 x Diesel generators / 29.880 kW
Propeller	4 x Rudder propeller
Bow thruster	2 x Brunvoll, Tunnel / each 2,400 kW

Figure 175: M/S Robin Hood   Photo: © TT-Line

Name of ship	M/S Robin Hood

Home port / Flag state	Lübeck / Germany
Shipyard / Yard number	Finnyards Oy, Rauma, Finland / #410
Previous ship names	-
Year of construction	1995

Call sign	DGDM	Classification	Germanischer Lloyd
IMO Number	9087465	MMSI Number	218370000
Length	179.71 m	Gross tonnage	26,796 GT
Beam	27.20 m	Net tonnage	11,589 NT
Draught	6.00 m	Deadweight	6,538 tdw
Passengers / Cabins	300 / 321	Maximum speed	19.5 kn
Vehicles	Unspecified	Cargo capacity	2,400 lm or 152 Lorries

Main engines	2 x MAK 6M552C, Diesel / each 6,500 kW
Auxiliary engines	4 x Diesel / each 4,500 kW
Propeller	2 x LIPS Fixed propeller
Bow thruster	2 x Tunnel / each 1,200 kW

Figure 176: M/S Tom Sawyer Photo: © TT-Line

| Name of ship | M/S Tom Sawyer | |

Home port / Flag state	Rostock / Germany
Shipyard / Yard number	Schichau Seebeckswerft, Bremerhaven, Germany/ #1064
Previous ship names	1989-1993 Robin Hood, 1993-2001 Nils Holgersson
Year of construction	1989

Call sign	DGRH	**Classification**	Germanischer Lloyd
IMO Number	8703232	**MMSI Number**	211149000
Length	177.20 m	**Gross tonnage**	26,391 GT
Beam	26.00 m	**Net tonnage**	8,417 NT
Draught	5.75 m	**Deadweight**	6,254 tdw
Passengers / Cabins	400 / 324	**Maximum speed**	19 kn
Vehicles	535 Cars	**Cargo capacity**	2,240 lm on 3 Decks

Main engines	2 x MAN B&W 8L40/45 / Diesel / each 3,170 kW 2 x MAN B&W 6L40/45 / Diesel / each 4,230 kW
Auxiliary engines	4 x Diesel / each 1,025 kW
Propeller	2 x Propeller, controllable pitch
Bow thruster	2 x KaMeWa, Tunnel

Figure 177: Routes Unity Line 2014   Photo and Graphic: © Unity Line

POLSTEAM Group

The Polish ferry operator Unity Line was launched in May 1994 with the claim, to become the "Best Ferry Company of the Baltic Sea". While this assessment may be very subjective, Unity Line succeeded to put into service in 1995 the M/S Polonia, at this time one of the most modern and safest Baltic ferries in service. Until today, the M/S Polonia is the flagship of Unity Line. As a result of the increasing demand, in 2008 followed the commissioning of the second RO/PAX ferry, the M/S Skania. Both ferries operate the route Świnoujście-Ystad / Ystad-Świnoujście. In the following years further five ferries were put into service, in contrast to the M/S Polonia and M/S Skania they were planned mainly for freight traffic and only secondary for passenger traffic. Between Świnoujście and Ystad these are the M/S Jan Śniadecki and the M/S Kopernik. With the M/S Galileusz, the M/S Gryf and the M/S Wolin the route network was extended with the ferry route Świnoujście / Trelleborg. [34]

Figure 178: M/S Gryf in the ferry terminal of Świnoujście (Poland)   Photo: © Unity Line

Figure 179: M/S Galileusz   Photo: © Unity Line

Name of ship	M/S Galileusz	

Home port / Flag state	Limassol / Cyprus
Shipyard / Yard number	Van der Giessen de Nord, Krimpen a/d Ijssel, Netherlands / #959
Previous ship names	1992-2006 Via Tirreno
Year of construction	1992

Call sign	C4LV2	Classification	Germanischer Lloyd
IMO Number	9019078	**MMSI Number**	210095000
Length	150.37 m	**Gross tonnage**	15,848 GT
Beam	23.40 m	**Net tonnage**	4,755 NT
Draught	5.90 m	**Deadweight**	6,710 tdw
Passengers / Cabins	128 / 51	**Maximum speed**	19.0 kn
Vehicles	Unspecified	**Cargo capacity**	90 Lorries / 1,650 lm

Main engines	2 x Zgoda 8ZAL40S, Diesel / each 5,760 kW
Auxiliary engines	2 x Diesel / each 1,000 kW
Propeller	2 x Propeller, controllable pitch
Bow thruster	2 x Tunnel / each 750 kW

Figure 180: M/S Gryf   Photo: © Unity Line

Name of ship   M/S Gryf   ▶━

Home port / Flag state	Nassau / Bahamas
Shipyard / Yard number	Bruce Shipyard, Landskrona, Sweden / #19, completed by Fosen Mekaniske Verksteder, Rissa, Norway / #43
Previous ship names	1991-2004 Kaptan Burhanettin Isim
Year of construction	1991

Call sign	C6TV9	**Classification**	Det Norske Veritas
IMO Number	8818300	**MMSI Number**	311794000
Length	157.90 m	**Gross tonnage**	18,653 GT
Beam	24.33 m	**Net tonnage**	5,595 NT
Draught	5.915 m	**Deadweight**	6,934 tdw
Passengers / Berths	180 / 144	**Maximum speed**	17.7 kn
Vehicles	Unspecified	**Cargo capacity**	1,800 lm

Main engines	2 x Sulzer 6ZA40S, Diesel / 7,920 kW
Auxiliary engines	3 x Mitsubishi S6R2 MPTK, Diesel
Propeller	2 x Propeller, controllable pitch Ulstein 95/4
Bow thruster	2 x Brunvoll FU63, Tunnel

Figure 181: M/S Jan Śniadecki   Photo: © Unity Line

Name of ship	M/S Jan Śniadecki	

Home port / Flag state	Limassol / Cyprus
Shipyard / Yard number	Falkenbergs Varv AB, Falkenberg, Sweden / #186
Previous ship names	-
Year of construction	1988

Call sign	P3TX6	Classification	Polski Rejestr Statkow
IMO Number	8604711	**MMSI Number**	212004000
Length	155.19 m	**Gross tonnage**	14,417 GT
Beam	21.60 m	**Net tonnage**	4,325 NT
Draught	5.10 m	**Deadweight**	5,149 tdw
Passengers / Berths	57 / 57	**Maximum speed**	19 kn
Vehicles	Unspecified	**Cargo capacity**	Main deck: 590.5 lm Upper deck : 487.0 lm

Main engines	4 x Zgoda Sulzer 6 ZL 40, Diesel / 11,840 kW
Auxiliary engines	Unspecified
Propeller	2 x Propeller, controllable pitch
Bow thruster	2 x Tunnel

Figure 182: M/S Kopernik   Photo: © Unity Line

Name of ship   M/S Kopernik

Home port / Flag state	Szczecin / Poland
Shipyard / Yard number	Bergens Mekaniske Verksted A/S,Bergen,Norway / #779
Previous ship names	1977-1999 Rostock, 1999-2005 Star Wind, 2005-2007 Vironia
Year of construction	1977

Call sign	5BXL3	**Classification**	Det Norske Veritas
IMO Number	7527887	**MMSI Number**	261449000
Length	160.07 m	**Gross tonnage**	14,221 GT
Beam	21.60 m	**Net tonnage**	4,266 NT
Draught	5.723 m	**Deadweight**	3,034 tdw
Passengers / Berths	360 / 119	**Maximum speed**	18 kn
Vehicles	75 Cars	**Cargo capacity**	5 Railway tracks track length 606 m

Main engines	4 x MAN B&W 8L40/54A, Diesel
Auxiliary engines	4 x SKL 8NVD 48A-2U, Diesel
Propeller	2 x Propeller, controllable pitch
Bow thruster	2 x Tunnel

Figure 183: M/S Polonia   Photo: © Unity Line

Name of ship	M/S Polonia	

Home port / Flag state	Nassau / Bahamas
Shipyard / Yard number	Langsten Slip & Båtbyggeri A/S, Tomrefjorden, Norway / #163
Previous ship names	-
Year of construction	1995

Call sign	C6NC7	Classification	Det Norske Veritas
IMO Number	9108350	MMSI Number	309272000
Length	169.90 m	Gross tonnage	29,875 GT
Beam	28.03 m	Net tonnage	10,582 NT
Draught	6.216 m	Deadweight	7,250 tdw
Passengers / Berths	918 / 618	Maximum speed	20.2 kn
Vehicles	808 lm Cars	Cargo capacity	2,777 lm Lorries

Main engines	4 x Wärtsilä 6SW38, Diesel / 21,840 kW
Auxiliary engines	3 x Wärtsilä 6SW280, Diesel
Propeller	2 x Propeller, controllable pitch Meckle
Bow thruster	3xBrunvoll SPA VP, Tunnel,1xStern thruster Brunvoll SPA VP

Figure 184: M/S Skania   Photo: © Unity Line

Name of ship   M/S Skania

Home port / Flag state	Nassau / Bahamas
Shipyard / Yard number	Schichau Seebeckwerft, Bremerhaven, Germany / #1087
Previous ship names	1995-2004 Superfast I, 2004-2008 Eurostar Roma
ear of construction	1995

Call sign	C6XF4	Classification	Det Norske Veritas
IMO Number	9086588	**MMSI Number**	311007200
Length	173.70 m	**Gross tonnage**	23,933 GT
Beam	24.00 m	**Net tonnage**	8,876 NT
Draught	6.419 m	**Deadweight**	5,717 tdw
Passengers / Berths	1,397 / 600	**Maximum speed**	27.0 kn
Vehicles	830 Cars	**Cargo capacity**	1,850 lm

Main engines	4 x Wärtsilä Italia 12ZA40S, Diesel / 34,550 kW
Auxiliary engines	3 x MAN 6L28/32A, Diesel
Propeller	2 x Propeller, controllable pitch 144 XF3/4-100 FO 156
Bow thruster	2 x KaMeWa 6L28/32A, Tunnel, Bow thruster 1 x ABB Zamech Marine CPT 1.75, Stern thruster

Figure 185: M/S Wolin   Photo: © Unity Line

Name of ship	M/S Wolin	

Home port / Flag state	Nassau / Bahamas
Shipyard / Yard number	Moss Fredrikstad Værft, Moss, Norway / #204
Previous ship names	1986-2002 Öresund, 2002-2007 Sky Wind
Year of construction	1986

Call sign	C6WN4	Classification	Det Norske Veritas
IMO Number	8420842	MMSI Number	309801000
Length	188.90 m	Gross tonnage	22,874 GT
Beam	23.10 m	Net tonnage	6,862 NT
Draught	5.90 m	Deadweight	5,143 tdw
Passengers / Berths	370 / 240	Maximum speed	18.0 kn
Vehicles	Unspecified	Cargo capacity	1,800 lm, 5 Railway Tracks with 650 m

Main engines	4 x MAN 6L40/45, Diesel / 13,200 kW
Auxiliary engines	2 x Wärtsilä 6R32BC, Diesel
Propeller	2 x Propeller, controllable pitch Liaaen EF115
Bow thruster	2 x Liaaen, Tunnel 1 x Liaaen TCN 105/75 250 (Stern thruster)

VIKING LINE

Today known as the Viking Line, this ferry operator was founded in 1966 as a merger of the three shipping companies Rederi Ab Ålandsfärjan, Rederi Ab Vikinglinjen and Rederi Ab Slite to compete in the Baltic traffic with Silja Line. Rederi Ab Ålandsfärjan 1970 changed its name to SF Line, the S stood for Sweden and the F stood for Finland in the name. In the same year, the former Rederi Ab Vikinglinjen was renamed in Rederi Ab Sally. As the owner of the company Silja Line, EffJohn, in 1987 took over Rederi Ab Sally, the Rederi Ab Sally was pressed from the other two shipping lines to leave the Viking Line. This left only two lines at the Viking Line organization. After the Rederi Ab Slite got into financial difficulties and had to declare bankruptcy in 1993, Viking Line de facto only consisted of the SF Line . Therefore, in the same year SF Line changed the name in Viking Line, under which still operates today. [35]

Figure 186: Viking Line in Helsinki   Photo: © Viking Line

Figure 187: M/S Amorella   Photo: © Viking Line

Name of ship	M/S Amorella	

Home port / Flag state	Mariehamn / Finland
Shipyard / Yard number	Brodogradilište Split, Split, Yugoslavia / #356
Previous ship names	-
Year of construction	1988

Call sign	OIWS	**Classification**	Det Norske Veritas
IMO Number	8601915	**MMSI Number**	230172000
Length	169.40 m	**Gross tonnage**	34,384 GT
Beam	28.20 m	**Net tonnage**	19,689 NT
Draught	6.35 m	**Deadweight**	3,690 tdw
Passengers	2,420	**Maximum speed**	21.5 kn
Vehicles	450 Cars	**Cargo capacity**	970 lm or 53 Lorries

Main engines	4 x Wärtsilä Pielstick 12PC26V-400, Diesel / 23,769 kW
Auxiliary engines	4 x Wärtsilä 6R32 BC, Diesel
Propeller	2 x Propeller, controllable pitch KaMeWa 157XF3/4
Bow thruster	2 x KaMeWa 2400D/AS-CP, Tunnel / 1,100 kW

Figure 188: M/S Gabriella   Photo: © Viking Line

Name of ship	M/S Gabriella	

Home port / Flag state	Mariehamn / Finland
Shipyard / Yard number	Brodogradiliste Split, Split, Croatia / #372
Previous ship names	1992-1994 Frans Suell, 1994-1997 Silja Scandinavica
Year of construction	1992

Call sign	OJHP	Classification	Det Norske Veritas
IMO Number	8917601	**MMSI Number**	230361000
Length	169.40 m	**Gross tonnage**	35,492 GT
Beam	28.20 m	**Net tonnage**	19,654 NT
Draught	6.368 m	**Deadweight**	2,962 tdw
Passengers / Berths	2,420 / 2,404	**Maximum speed**	20.5 kn
Vehicles	400 Cars	**Cargo capacity**	970 lm

Main engines	4 x Pielstick-Wärtsilä 12 PC2-6/2V, Diesel / 23,780 kW
Auxiliary engines	4 x Wärtsilä 6R32BC, Diesel
Propeller	2 x Propeller, controllable pitch KaMeWa 157XF3/4RF
Bow thruster	2 x KaMeWa, Tunnel

Figure 189: M/S Mariella   Photo: © Viking Line

Name of ship	M/S Mariella	

Home port / Flag state	Mariehamn / Finland
Shipyard / Yard number	Oy Wärtsilä Ab, Åbo, Finland / #1286
Previous ship names	-
Year of construction	1985

Call sign	OITI	Classification	Det Norske Veritas
IMO Number	8320573	**MMSI Number**	230181000
Length	175.70 m	**Gross tonnage**	37,860 GT
Beam	28.40 m	**Net tonnage**	24,421 NT
Draught	6.78 m	**Deadweight**	3,524 tdw
Passengers / Berths	2,447 / 2,447	**Maximum speed**	22 kn
Vehicles	580 Cars	**Cargo capacity**	1,115 lm

Main engines	4 x Pielstick-Wärtsilä 12PC2-6V-400, Diesel / 23,000 kW
Auxiliary engines	3 x Wärtsilä 6R32BC, Diesel
Propeller	2 x Propeller, controllable pitch Fischer 157S4
Bow thruster	2 x KaMeWa 2400AS/CP

Figure 190: M/S Rosella   Photo: © Viking Line

Name of ship	M/S Rosella	

Home port / Flag state	Mariehamn / Finland
Shipyard / Yard number	Oy Wärtsilä AB, Åbo, Finland / #1249
Previous ship names	-
Year of construction	1980

Call sign	SDEV	Classification	Det Norske Veritas
IMO Number	7901265	**MMSI Number**	266296000
Length	136.11 m	**Gross tonnage**	16,879 GT
Beam	24.24 m	**Net tonnage**	5,063 NT
Draught	5.40 m	**Deadweight**	2,300 tdw
Passengers / Berths	1,530 / 1,184	**Maximum speed**	21.5 kn
Vehicles	350 Cars	**Cargo capacity**	720 lm or 43 Trailers

Main engines	4 x Pielstick-Wärtsilä 12PC2-2V 400, Diesel / 17,760 kW
Auxiliary engines	4 x Wärtsilä 824 TS, Diesel
Propeller	2 x Propeller, controllable pitch KaMeWa 2X121XF/4
Bow thruster	2 x KaMeWa 1650/AS-CP/59, Tunnel

Figure 191: M/S Viking Cinderella   Photo: © Viking Line

Name of ship   M/S Viking Cinderella

Home port / Flag state	Stockholm / Sweden
Shipyard / Yard number	Wärtsilä Marine Industries, Turku Shipyard, Turku, Finland / #1302
Previous ship names	1989-2003 Cinderella
Year of construction	1989

Call sign	SEAI	Classification	Det Norske Veritas
IMO Number	8719188	MMSI Number	266027000
Length	191.00 m	Gross tonnage	46,398 GT
Beam	35.84 m	Net tonnage	29,223 NT
Draught	6.60 m	Deadweight	4,228 tdw
Passengers	2,560	Maximum speed	21 kn
Vehicles	100 Cars	Cargo capacity	760 lm

Main engines	4 x Wärtsilä-Sulzer 12ZAV 40S ER1, Diesel / 28,800 kW
Auxiliary engines	4 x Wärtsilä 6R32E, Diesel
Propeller	2 x Propeller, controllable pitch KaMeWa 171 XF3/4
Bow thruster	2 x KaMeWa 2400D/AS-CP, Tunnel

Figure 192: M/S Viking Grace   Photo: © Viking Line

Name of ship	M/S Viking Grace	

Home port / Flag state	Mariehamn / Finland
Shipyard / Yard number	STX Finland, Perno, Finland / #1376
Previous ship names	-
Year of construction	2013

Call sign	OJPQ	Classification	Lloyd's Register of Shipping
IMO Number	9606900	**MMSI Number**	230629000
Length	218.00 m	**Gross tonnage**	57,565 GT
Beam	31.80 m	**Net tonnage**	37,600 NT
Draught	6.80 m	**Deadweight**	5,030 tdw
Passengers / Cabins	2,800 / 880	**Maximum speed**	21.8 kn
Vehicles	100 Cars+500 lm extra car deck	**Cargo capacity**	1,250 lm

Main engines	4 x Wärtsilä 8L50DF, optional Diesel or LNG / each 7,600 kW
Auxiliary engines	2 x 10,500 kW
Propeller	2 x 5-Blatt-Festpropeller
Bow thruster	2 x Bow thruster each 2,300 kW, 1 x Stern thruster 1,500 kW

Figure 193: M/S Viking XPRS   Photo: © Viking Line

Name of ship	M/S Viking XPRS	

Home port / Flag state	Norrtälje / Sweden
Shipyard / Yard number	Aker Finnyards, Helsinki, Finland / #1358
Previous ship names	-
Year of construction	2008

Call sign	SBXN	Classification	Lloyd's Register of Shipping
IMO Number	9375654	MMSI Number	265611110
Length	185.00 m	Gross tonnage	35,778 GT
Beam	27.70 m	Net tonnage	14,165 NT
Draught	6.55 m	Deadweight	5,184 tdw
Passengers / Cabins	2,500 / 238	Maximum speed	25 kn
Vehicles	230 Cars	Cargo capacity	1,000 lm or 60 Lorries

Main engines	4 x Wärtsilä 8L46F, Diesel / 40,000 kW
Auxiliary engines	Unspecified
Propeller	2 x Propeller, controllable pitch
Bow thruster	2 x Tunnel

Wasaline (Finland)

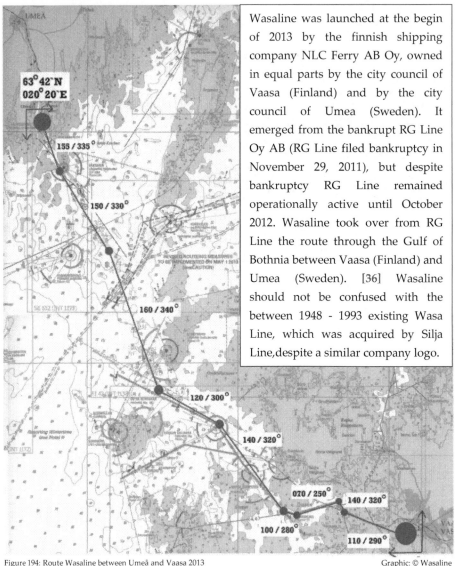

Wasaline was launched at the begin of 2013 by the finnish shipping company NLC Ferry AB Oy, owned in equal parts by the city council of Vaasa (Finland) and by the city council of Umea (Sweden). It emerged from the bankrupt RG Line Oy AB (RG Line filed bankruptcy in November 29, 2011), but despite bankruptcy RG Line remained operationally active until October 2012. Wasaline took over from RG Line the route through the Gulf of Bothnia between Vaasa (Finland) and Umea (Sweden). [36] Wasaline should not be confused with the between 1948 - 1993 existing Wasa Line, which was acquired by Silja Line,despite a similar company logo.

Figure 194: Route Wasaline between Umeå and Vaasa 2013   Graphic: © Wasaline

Wasaline owned in 2013 only one ship, the M/S "Wasa Express", which was used in scheduled service between the Swedish port of Umeå and Vaasa in Finland. Wasaline offers crossings as well as thematic mini cruises and conference tours. The business concept is completed by the use of the ship for additional cargo business.

Figure 195: M/S Wasa Express   Photo: © Wasaline

Name of ship	M/S Wasa Express	

Home port / Flag state	Vaasa / Finland
Shipyard /Yard number	Oy Wärtsilä AB, Helsinki, Finland / #432
Previous ship names	1981-1987 Travemünde, 1987-1988 Travemünde Link, 1988-1997 Sally Star,1997 Wasa Express, 1997-2004 / 2006-2007/ 2010-2011 Thjelvar, 2004-2006 Color Traveller, 2007-2010 Rostock, 2011-2012 Betancuria
Year of construction	1981

Call sign	OJQB	**Classification**	Det Norske Veritas
IMO Number	8000226	**MMSI Number**	230636000
Length	141.00 m	**Gross tonnage**	17,053 GT
Beam	22.81 m	**Net tonnage**	7,729 NT
Draught	4.95 m	**Deadweight**	4,150 tdw
Passengers / Cabins	1,500 / 316	**Maximum speed**	19.5 kn
Vehicles	450 Cars	**Cargo capacity**	1,150 lm

Main engines	4 x Wärtsilä 12V32 4SA, Diesel / 14,840 kW
Auxiliary engines	2 x Wärtsilä 4I32
Propeller	2 x KaMeWa Propeller, controllable pitch
Bow thruster	1 x KaMeWa 2000AS-CP

Figure 196: Outside environment on Colorline ferry   Photo: © Robert Dreier Tveit Holand

5.	Definitions	

Abbrev.	Term	Definition
	Auxiliary engines	Engines for additional power and electric energy
	Beam	Breadth in metres
	Berths	Number of available berths
	Bow thruster	Maneuvering unit (engine + propeller) for ship movements sidewards, mounted in front bow
	Cabins	Number of available cabins
	Call Sign	Marine radio code, individual for every vessel, first character is country code + in general 3 digits assigned from the national authorities
	Cargo capacity	Loading capacity in lane metres, tons or specified with number of trucks or trailers
	Classification	Classif. society (responsable for certification)
	Deadweight	Ship's carrying capacity with crew and supplies, measured in tdw (tons deadweight)
	Draught	depth below water line to the bottom of the hull of the ship (in metres)
	Flag state	Country of ship registration
GT	Gross Tonnage	Defined as the moulded volume of all enclosed spaces of the ship
HSC	High Speed Catamaran	High speed vessel with double hull
	Home port	Registered home port of the vessel, corrispond with flag state
IMO	International Maritime Organisation	
	IMO Number	IMO designated number for ship identification, number do not change in all the ship lifetime
Kn	Knots	Naut. unit for measure speed 1 kn = 1,852 m/h
kW	Kilowatt	Unit for measure power output of engines
Lm	Lane meter	Unit for measure cargo space on Ro-Ro ships
	Length	Length over all of the ship in metres
	Main engines	Main propulsion engines, connected with shaft and propeller, waterjets or propulsion nacelles
	Maximum speed	Maximum speed in Knots
M	Metre	Metric unit for measure length

Abbrev.	Term	Definition
MMSI	Maritime Mobile Service Identity	
	MMSI Number	nine digit code ,sended over radio frequency channel in order to identify ship stations
M/S	Motorship	Vessel with engine propulsion
NT	Net Tonnage	index calculated from the total moulded volume of the ship's cargo spaces
	Passengers	Number of passengers
	Previous ship names	Previous names of the ship since commissioning
	Propeller	Rotating multiple bladed device, that turn on a shaft, used for propulsion purposes
	Propulsion nacelles	Enclosed propulsion unit, swivelling for maneuvering
SOLAS	Safety of Life at Sea	International Convention for the Safety of Life at Sea, international maritime safety treaty
	Service Speed	Average speed under normal load and weather conditions
	Shipyard	Ship builder
	Stern thruster	Maneuvering unit (engine + propeller) for ship movements sidewards, mounted in stern
tdw	Tons deadweight	Unit for measure deadweight
	Vehicles	Number of cars on board
	Waterjet	Propulsion system by a jet of water, consists in general of a ducted propeller with nozzle
	Yard number	Number, designated from the shipyard
	Year of construction	Year of completion of the vessel

Figure 197: Ferry port of Puttgarden (Germany) Photo: © Scandlines

Figure 198: Caravans on ferry deck / TT-Line ferry M/S Robin Hood passing   Photo: © TT-Line

7.	References	Page
[1]	Accident Investigation Board Norway: REPORT ON THE INVESTIGATION OF A MARINE ACCIDENT NORDLYS LHCW - FIRE ON BOARD DURING APPROACH TO ÅLESUND-15 SEPTEMBER 2013, REPORT Sjø 2013/02, Issued May 2013	15
[2]	Niclas Meyer - Bachelorarbeit: Unfalluntersuchung zur starken Kraengung der LISCO GLORIA durch den Einfluss von Loeschwasser auf dem Hauptfahrzeugdeck, TUHH, Institut fuer Entwerfen von Schiffen und Schiffssicherheit Prof. Dr.-Ing. Stefan Krueuger, 30/04/2012	16
[3]	Joint Accident Investigation Commission of Estonia, Finland and Sweden (1995) : "Part Report on MV Estonia", April 1995	16
[4]	European Court of Human Rights, CASE OF BRUDNICKA AND OTHERS v. POLAND (Application no. 54723/00), Judgement, Strasbourg, 3 March 2005, Final 03/06/2005	17
[5]	Safety: http://eurotestmobility.hades.webhouse.dk/wp-content/uploads/2014/07/Tips-for-passengers-FINAL.pdf	17
[6]	SOLAS rules for evacuation of ferries MSC Circ 1283	17
[7]	Report about detention of the "Norman Voyager" http://news.bbc.co.uk/2/hi/uk_news/england/hampshire/8371469.stm	21
[8]	Joint Accident Investigation Commission of Estonia, Finland and Sweden (1995) : "Part Report on MV Estonia", April 1995	21
[9]	Joint Accident Investigation Commission of Estonia, Finland and Sweden (1995) : "Part Report on MV Estonia", April 1995	21
[10]	Hans-Hermann Diestel: Seeunfälle und Schiffssicherheit in der Ostsee, Hinstorff-Verlag GmbH, Rostock, 2013	21
[11]	Website Brittany Ferries: http://www.brittany-ferries.co.uk/information/about-brittany-ferries	25
[12]	Website Color Line AS: http://www.colorline.de/service/konzerngeschichte	36
[13]	Website Condor Ferries: http://www.condorferries.co.uk/about.aspx	43
[14]	Website DFDS: http://www.dfdsseaways.co.uk/about-us/	47
[15]	Web LD Lines: http://www.ldline.co.uk as part of http://www.ferryto.co.uk	47
[16]	Website Rederi AB, Eckerö: http://www.rederiabeckero.ax/	67
[17]	Website Eckerö Linjen: https://www.eckerolinjen.se/en/	67
[18]	Website Eckerö Line: http://www.eckeroline.fi	67
[19]	Website Færgen: http://www.faergen.dk/info/om-faergen.aspx	70
[20]	Website Finnlines: http://www.finnlines.com/company/business_areas	84
[21]	Website Finnlines: http://m.finnlines.com/en/%28nid%29/6715	84
[22]	Website Wikipedia: http://de.wikipedia.org/wiki/Fjord_Line	93
[23]	Web Hurtigruten: http://www.hurtigruten.co.uk/utils/About-Hurtigruten/History/120-years-of-coastal-voyages/	98
[24]	Web Irish Continental Group: http://www.icg.ie/irish-continental-group-history.asp	110
[25]	Website Moby SPL Line: http://www.stpeterline.com/about, http://de.wikipedia.org/wiki/St._Peter_Line#cite_note-2	113
[26]	Website P&O Heritage: http://www.poheritage.com/about-po-ferries	115
[27]	Website Polferries: http://www.polferries.pl/prom/o_nas/historia	125
[28]	Website Scandlines: http://www.scandlines.de/uber-scandlines/uber-scandlines-titelseite/unternehmensgeschichte.aspx	129

[29]	Michael Meyer: 3i und Allianz einigen sich über Ausstieg bei Scandlines. In: Täglicher Hafenbericht vom 6. November 2013, S. 1/4	129
[30]	Website Smyril Line: http://www.smyrilline.com/about-us-11408.aspx	140
[31]	Website Stena Line: http://www.stenaline.com/en/stena-line/corporate/	142
[32]	Website Tallink-Silja Line: http://www.tallink.com/about	165
[33]	Website TT Line: http://www.ttline.com/de/Germany/TT-Line/Unternehmensprofil/Chronik/	177
[34]	Website Unity Line: http://www.unityline.eu/page/unity-line/about-unity-line	184
[35]	Website Viking Line: http://www.vikingline.com/en/Investors-and-the-Group/History/	192
[36]	Website Wikipedia: http://en.wikipedia.org/wiki/Wasa_Line	200

Figure 199: Stena ferries – encounter

Photo: © Stena Line

31263720R00119

Made in the USA
Middletown, DE
29 December 2018